Best Easy Day Hikes
Birmingham

Help Us Keep This Guide Up to Date

Every effort has been made by the author and editors to make this guide as accurate and useful as possible; however, many things can change after a guide is published—regulations change, facilities come under new management, and so forth.

We would love to hear from you concerning your experiences with this guide and how you feel it could be improved and kept up to date. While we may not be able to respond to all comments and suggestions, we'll take them to heart, and we'll also make certain to share them with the author. Please send your comments and suggestions to falconeditorial@rowman.com.

Thanks for your input!

Best Easy Day Hikes Series

Best Easy Day Hikes
Birmingham

Joe Cuhaj

FALCONGUIDES

ESSEX, CONNECTICUT

FALCONGUIDES®

An imprint of Globe Pequot, the trade division of
The Rowman & Littlefield Publishing Group, Inc.
4501 Forbes Blvd., Ste. 200
Lanham, MD 20706
www.rowman.com

Falcon and FalconGuides are registered trademarks and Make Adventure Your
Story is a trademark of The Rowman & Littlefield Publishing Group, Inc.

Distributed by NATIONAL BOOK NETWORK

British Library Cataloguing in Publication Information Available

Library of Congress Cataloging in Publication Data

Names: Cuhaj, Joe author.
Title: Best easy day hikes Birmingham / Joe Cuhaj.
Description: Essex, Connecticut : FalconGuides, [2023] | Series: Best easy
    day hikes series
Identifiers: LCCN 2022052413 (print) | LCCN 2022052414 (ebook) | ISBN
    9781493070190 (paperback) | ISBN 9781493070206 (epub)
Subjects: LCSH: Day hiking–Alabama–Birmingham Region–Guidebooks. |
    Trails–Alabama–Birmingham Region–Guidebooks. | Birmingham Region
    (Ala.)–Guidebooks.
Classification: LCC GV199.42.A22 B573 2023 (print) | LCC GV199.42.A22
    (ebook) | DDC 796.5109761/781–dc23/eng/20221104
LC record available at https://lccn.loc.gov/2022052413
LC ebook record available at https://lccn.loc.gov/2022052414

♾™ The paper used in this publication meets the minimum requirements of
American National Standard for Information Sciences—Permanence of Paper for
Printed Library Materials, ANSI/NISO Z39.48-1992.

Contents

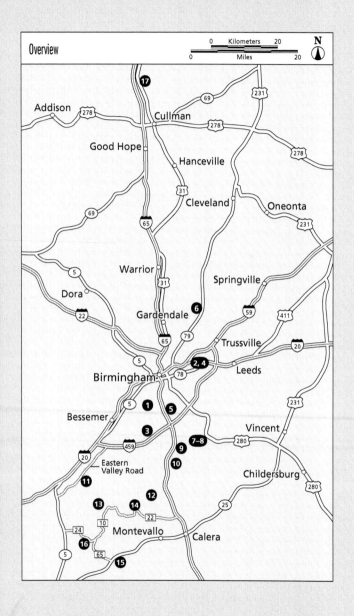

Introduction

Like all cities, the *Magic City*, Birmingham, Alabama, can be a maddening place: Rush hour traffic can be nerve wracking, constant road work can be frustrating, but underlying all the hustle and bustle of any major city, there is another world. It's a world of beauty where you can climb to the heights of a rock outcropping and lose yourself in the views, where you can soothe your soul in the roar of a waterfall, and where nature provides solace from the trials of everyday life.

Welcome to the natural side of Birmingham. Across this region, preserves and county, state, and historic parks offer you the chance to get away from it all and get lost in the wonder of nature, but the only way to get there is by taking a hike. That's what this book is all about—taking you on some of the best easy day hikes in the Birmingham area.

The hikes described within these pages will guide you to churning waterfalls, the city's mining history that led to its moniker of the "Magic City," enchanting swamps with teeming wildlife, and fun hikes that kids of all ages will love and that will get them interested in the great outdoors.

I hope you enjoy the journeys I have presented and they will inspire you to expand your horizon and explore the hundreds of other amazing hikes across Alabama.

Weather

The best time for hiking in Birmingham is from late September to late April. These are the coolest months of the year. After that, the combination of summer heat and humidity can be oppressive. Now don't get me wrong. The summer months do have their cool spells, but they are short lived.

Fall ignites glorious colors in the hardwoods across the area's mountains with high temperatures averaging in the mid-60s. In winter, don't be surprised by a light dusting to a few inches of snow on the ground. Winter high temperatures average around 54 degrees.

In spring as the wildflowers bloom and brighten the trails, the average high temperature is 60 degrees, the perfect hiking weather. Spring, however, is also known for bringing severe weather to the South, including outbreaks of strong and dangerous thunderstorms and tornadoes. Keep an eye on the weather before heading out.

Keep in mind that waterfalls and small streams are seasonal in Alabama and may not be flowing in the heat of summer.

Critters

The most common animals you will see on the trail include whitetail deer and wild turkey. Birds abound and I try to give you an idea of the species you may see in the trail descriptions. You may also come across bobcat, coyote, and black bear, but they are rare.

You will undoubtedly encounter snakes. Watch where you step and where you place your hands clambering over rocks and logs for cottonmouth along the rivers and streams and rattlesnakes in the brush.

Be Prepared

Even though these are only day hikes of short to moderately long distances, you still need to be prepared:

- Always carry and drink plenty of water or sport drinks with electrolytes. Also, learn how to recognize the signs of heat stroke or exhaustion and how to treat it.

- Be sure to pack snacks such as granola bars or trail mix or a lunch to help keep your energy up.
- The sun can be unforgiving. Wear a hat and slather on the sunscreen.
- Don't forget the insect spray. They can be ferocious around waterways in warm weather.
- Don't pick or touch flowers or foliage. Poison ivy and other nasty rash-inducing plants are hidden out there.

Leave No Trace

As trail users, it is our responsibility to be vigilant when on the trail to make sure we leave the trail undisturbed and we leave no trace of our visit. When on the trail, please follow these simple Leave No Trace rules:

- Pack out all your trash and if possible, bring along a small garbage bag and pick up trash you may find along the trail.
- Do not approach or feed wild animals. They can be dangerous and feeding them causes them to lose self-reliance in the wild.
- Don't pick wildflowers, gather rocks, or take any historical artifacts you may find.
- Don't create shortcuts or switchbacks by walking off trail to cut corners. This leads to erosion.
- Do not make loud noises.
- Use outhouses at the trailhead or as found along the trail.

How to Use This Guide

The trails selected for this guide all fall within a one-hour drive from the center of the city, so no matter where you find yourself in Birmingham, you can take a quick getaway to rejuvenate yourself in nature.

For the most part, the hikes are easy to moderate in difficulty. There are three exceptions: Hike #7 King's Chair Loop, #10 Peavine Falls Loop, and #17 Hurricane Creek Park. These three are rated moderate to difficult.

All hikes are less than 5 miles in length with the exception of Hike #1 Red Mountain Park, which is 5.4 miles.

Selecting a Hike

Remember, "easy" is a relative term. "Easy" takes on a different meaning if you are hiking with small children, if you are a bit out of shape or haven't walked a trail in a while, or if it's extremely hot outside. This guide will allow you to make the best decision about what trails you should tackle.

Each hike has a difficulty classification:

- Easy: Short, relatively flat trails that take no more than an hour to complete, two at most.
- Moderate: Longer distance, more challenging terrain.
- Difficult: Steep stretches or difficult obstacles to navigate.

Approximate hiking times are based on the distance and the pace an average person can walk (2 to 2.5 miles per hour). This time does not include stopping for breaks, taking photographs, or just relaxing and taking in the landscapes.

Trail Finder

The following lists the trails covered from easiest to difficult. Asterisks indicate the trail is ADA accessible, depending on weather:

Easy

12	Ebenezer Swamp Ecological Preserve ★
5	Boulder Canyon Nature Trail
9	Treetop Trail / Alabama Wildlife Center ★ (Boardwalk only ADA accessible)
4	Ruffner Mountain Wetlands
8	Maggie's Glen Loop
15	Furnace Trail
13	Reflection Trail
11	Tannehill Ironworks Historical State Park
6	Turkey Creek Nature Preserve

Easy to Moderate

2	Ruffner Mountain Nature Preserve
3	Moss Rock Preserve

Moderate

14	Falling Rock Falls
16	Piper Interpretive Trail
1	Red Mountain Park

Moderate to Difficult

10	Peavine Falls Loop
17	Hurricane Creek Park
7	King's Chair Loop

Map Legend

65	Interstate Highway
31	US Highway
97	State Highway
	Local Road
	Unpaved Road
	Featured Trail
	Trail
	Boardwalk/Stairs
	River/Creek
	Body of Water
	Marsh/Swamp
	State Park/Preserve/Wetlands
	Bench
	Bridge
▲	Camping
•─•	Gate
❷	Information Center
℗	Parking
▲	Peak
	Picnic Area
■	Point of Interest/Structure
	Restroom
⚬	Spring
○	Town
❶❶	Trailhead
	Viewpoint/Overlook
	Waterfall

1 Red Mountain Park

Once a major iron-ore mining site, Red Mountain is now a beautiful and extremely popular 1,500-acre park that teaches visitors about the rich mining history of Birmingham. Choose from a series of fun, scenic, and sometimes challenging trails that weave their way past long since abandoned historic mines, mine cars, and hoist houses with beautiful overlooks along the way.

Start: Trailhead on Frankfurt Drive
Distance: 5.4-mile loop
Hiking time: About 3 hours
Difficulty: Moderate
Trail surface: Dirt footpath, gravel road
Best season: Sept through Apr
Other trail users: Cyclists, walkers, joggers
Canine compatibility: Leashed dogs permitted

Land status: City park
Schedule: Year-round, 7 a.m. to 5 p.m.
Fees and permits: None
Maps: USGS maps: Bessemer, Bessemer Iron District, Birmingham South, Alabama
Contact: Red Mountain Park, 283 Lyon Lane, Birmingham 35211; (205) 202-6043; www.redmountainpark.org

Finding the trailhead: From I-65 in Birmingham, take exit 255 and head west on West Lakeshore Parkway. Travel 3 miles and turn right onto Frankfurt Drive. Travel 0.5 mile. The trailhead is at the bend as Frankfurt Drive becomes Lyon Lane. Park along Frankfurt Drive.
Trailhead GPS: N33 26.712' / W86 51.753'

The Hike

To make Birmingham the industrial powerhouse it was in the 1800s and the bustling city it is today, it took a little red dust—iron ore. Red Mountain Park gives hikers a chance to visit that part of the city's history and learn about the sweat and backbreaking work it took to bring the ore to market.

In the 1840s, local farmer Baylis Earle Grace identified the dust as hematite (iron ore) and began scraping the land and shipping the material to a foundry in a neighboring county. As the Civil War approached, speculators began buying up large tracts of land on and near Red Mountain with the goal of capitalizing on the now-burgeoning iron-mining industry. The area's first commercial mine, known as Eureka 1, was opened in 1863 (the mine is located on the eastern side of the park). And with that the mining boom was on, the population increased, and in 1871 the city of Birmingham was founded.

The last active mine on the mountain was closed in 1962 by its owner at the time, US Steel. After that Red Mountain stood virtually untouched until 2007 when—through the efforts of Ervin Battain, the work of many volunteers, and an amazingly generous donation by US Steel of its 1,500 acres of land on the mountain—the vision to create a historic park was born.

Today, the park boasts more than 15 miles of hiking trails, most being dirt and rock footpaths with the remainder being old gravel mining roads and railroad beds. The trails interconnect, allowing you to create your own loop adventures. The hike described here takes you to two beautiful overlooks, three historic iron mines (which are sealed off), and hoist houses.

The trailhead is located on a bend in the road where Frankfurt Drive becomes Lyon Lane. You can park anywhere along the side of Frankfurt Drive. Be forewarned: This is one popular park and can be very crowded on weekends. You may have to park a good 0.75 mile from the trailhead. The good news is that this loop takes you away from the crowd.

The loop described here uses several different trails to make the circuit. The Ike Maston and Smythe Trails are labeled as being "most difficult" by the park with long, steep, rocky grades, but you'll be heading downhill. It can be tough on the knees but manageable and much better than if you hiked uphill.

Highlights of the hike are visits to the #13 Mine Trail and Ishkooda Mine #14, and the Redding Shaft Mine and Hoist House that you will find near the intersection of the Songo and Ike Maston Trails. The electric-powered hoist house helped haul the ore from the mine and is a beautiful mission-style structure.

Miles and Directions

0.0 Start at the trailhead on Frankfort Drive to the north on the gravel path. In less than 0.1 mile come to a Y. Take the right fork.

0.2 Cross a 40-foot bridge and arrive at Remy's Dog Park.

0.3 Come to a T intersection with a wide gravel road. Turn right (east) onto the road.

0.4 Come to an intersection. The Schaeffer Spectacles, a giant sculpture of eyeglasses donated by a park sponsor, are at the junction as well as a welcome kiosk and portable restrooms. Turn right (north) onto the #13 Mine Trail. In less than 0.1 mile, pass a side trail on the right that leads to a picnic area.

0.6 Pass a Boy Scout hammock area on the right. In less than 0.1 mile, come to an intersection with a gravel road. Turn right onto the gravel road to the northeast heading toward the Adventure Area, then walking around the area on the right side. At the storage unit located here there is a Y. A sign here shows the Eureka Mines is to the left (northeast), the BMRR South Trail to the right. Take the left fork and head to the Eureka Mines.

0.9 Pass a bridge on the right (you'll come back to that in a moment) and continue straight to the northwest to visit the #13 Mine. When done, retrace your steps back to the bridge and turn left crossing the bridge to the east onto the Ike Maston Trail.

1.3 Turn left (north) onto the #14 Mine Spur Trail. The trail narrows to a 2-foot-wide rock and dirt path.

1.4 Arrive at the Ishkooda Mine #14. When done exploring, retrace your steps and in less than 0.1 mile turn left (southeast) onto the Redding/Ishkooda Trail.

1.7 Turn left (southwest) onto the rocky, wide Ishkooda Trail.

1.8 Pass old cement mining structures. A tall rock bluff begins on the left.

2.0 Pass the foundation of a hoist house on the right. In less than 0.1 mile pass a bench on the right, bluffs on the left.

2.1 Pass the Mine #13 Bridge on the left.

2.2 Arrive at the Protective Life Picnic Area and an intersection of several trails. Continue to the southwest on the Ishkooda Overlook Connector. In less than 0.1 mile, a trail branches to the right at a sign that reads, "stay on the trail." Take the left fork onto the Skyhy Ridge Trail.

2.4 The trail narrows again to a 2- to 3-foot-wide rocky path atop a narrow ridge with long and steep drops to either side.

2.5 Climb down a short set of railroad tie stairs. You will start to see a bit of the city to your right through the trees.

2.6 Pass between two small cement foundations.

2.7 Pass a foundation and steel I-beams on the right. Climb down a short set of railroad-tie stairs.

3.0 Arrive at the Ishkooda Overlook with a picnic table and a view of the Birmingham suburbs. Grab a snack, enjoy the

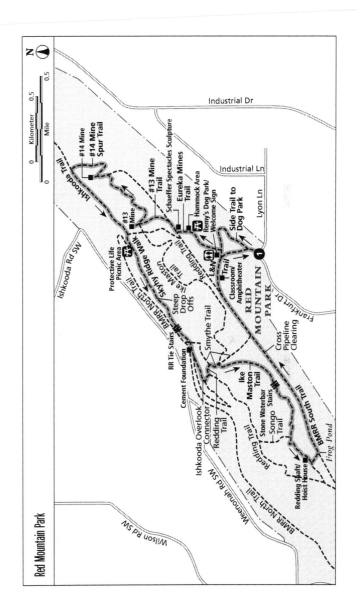

Red Mountain Park

view, then backtrack just a few yards and turn right (southeast) onto a short connector trail. In less than 0.1 mile, come to an intersection and turn left (northeast) onto the Redding Trail.

3.1 Come to the intersection with the Smythe Trail that bears off to the right and straight. Continue straight to the southeast on the Smythe Trail.

3.2 Turn right (west) onto the Ike Maston Trail.

3.3 Pass a view of the valley on your left.

3.5 Cross an intermittent stream with a stone water bar. After crossing, climb a hill to the west on some old wooden stairs made from railroad ties.

3.8 The Songo Trail joins the Ike Maston Trail from the right (north). Continue straight to the northwest on the Ike Maston Trail. In a few hundred feet, cross a stream over a nice wooden bridge.

4.0 Arrive at the Redding Shaft Mine and Hoist House. There are informational signs describing their history. Turn left (southeast) onto the Songo Trail, which is now a gravel and dirt road.

4.1 Turn left (northeast) onto the BMRR South Trail. A frog pond is here at the bend and the frog song is marvelous in the late evening.

4.7 Cross a clearing for a petroleum pipeline.

4.8 Pass the Smythe Trail on the left.

5.0 Pass the Ike Maston Trail on the left. In less than 0.1 mile, come to a Y. Take the right fork to the east onto the L&N Trail.

5.1 Pass a small outdoor classroom/amphitheater on the right.

5.2 Arrive back at the information kiosk from mile 0.4. Turn right to the southeast to head back to the trailhead.

5.4 Arrive back at the trailhead.

2 Ruffner Mountain Nature Preserve

This loop hike will use the preserve's backbone trail, the Quarry Trail, and several of its spurs to explore the mountain's amazing history as we pay visits to a quarry, a giant ore crusher hidden away in the forest, an overlook or two, and many wildflowers.

Start: From the north side of the Ruffner Mountain Nature Center parking lot beneath the wooden archway at the trailhead entrance

Distance: 4.6-mile out-and-back with two loops

Hiking time: About 2.5 hours

Difficulty: Easy to moderate

Trail surface: Dirt and rock

Best season: Winter to early summer

Other trail users: None

Canine compatibility: Dogs permitted; leash required

Land status: Nonprofit nature center

Schedule: Tues through Sun 7 a.m. to 5 p.m. Nov through Feb, 7 a.m. to 7 p.m. remainder of the year; closed Mon

Fees and permits: A parking pass is required. It may be purchased at the pavilion near the nature center or by the parking app (use the QR code on-site to pay). An alternative, and one that helps the preserve continue its mission, is to become a member, which includes a yearly parking pass. See the website under Contact.

Maps: USGS Irondale, AL; trail maps available at trailhead kiosk

Contact: Ruffner Mountain Nature Center, 1214 81st St., Birmingham 35206; (205) 833-8264; www.ruffnermountain.org

Special considerations: When the parking lot is full, no other vehicles will be allowed into the park. If the parking lot is closed, do not park on 81st Street. You will be ticketed or towed.

Finding the trailhead: From Birmingham from the intersection of I-59 and 1st Avenue North in Birmingham, take exit 132. In 0.3 mile, merge onto 1st Avenue North and in 300 feet, turn right onto 83rd Street North. Travel 0.9 mile and turn left onto 81st Street South. Travel 0.5 mile and turn left onto 81st Alley Street. In 100 feet, you will arrive at the parking loop. The trailhead begins next to the nature center. **Trailhead GPS:** N33 33.516' / W86 42.429'

The Hike

Ruffner Mountain Nature Preserve was established in 1977 with the mission to connect Birmingham's residents and visitors to the area's natural beauty, fostering an appreciation for nature and living things in the busy metropolitan area.

Opening with only 28 acres of land, the preserve has since grown to encompass over 1,000 acres of wetlands and hardwood forest. The preserve also protects a bit of the area's rich mining history, which you will see along this hike.

Over the years, volunteers have carved out over 12 miles of trails that allow you to explore this oasis in the middle of the bustling city. The main trail that connects them all, the backbone of the trail system, is the Quarry Trail. The white-blazed trail runs the length of the southern end of Ruffner Mountain. Many spur trails split off the trail leading hikers to overlooks and the mountain's mining past. You will be using the Quarry Trail and a few of its spurs to make this trek through the preserve.

The hike is easy to moderate in difficulty with a few short climbs. The climbs uphill are made a bit easier in many spots with stone steps. Overall, the trails have a dirt and rock bed that can be muddy after a good, hard rain. From spring through early fall, the canopy is very thick, providing excellent shade in the hot Southern summer.

The trails at Ruffner Mountain have excellent blazing and getting lost is virtually impossible. All intersections have unique wooden signs pointing the direction to each trail. Along the Quarry Trail, you will learn about the plants, trees, and animals of the area through the many descriptive interpretive signs that dot the path.

This hike is highlighted with a visit to an old iron ore crusher that appears out of nowhere as you hike the Crusher Trail. You will also make stops at the deep limestone quarry and take in views from Cambrian Overlook and Hawkeye Overlook.

Use caution on the bluffs and overlooks. They are steep, so keep your kids and dogs at hand. There are trails that lead down into the quarry, but they are very steep and can be dangerous. This hike will simply rim the quarry for excellent views.

Miles and Directions

0.0 Start from the north side of the parking lot under the wooden trailhead archway next to the nature center. The Quarry Trail is blazed white.

0.1 Cross over a paved road to the south. An information kiosk is on the other side with a lockbox for donations. Continue straight on the Quarry Trail.

0.3 Come to Miner's Junction. A sign here points the direction of the Quarry and Crusher Trails. Turn left here (south) onto the Crusher Trail.

0.4 Cross over the orange-blazed Ridge and Valley Trail to the east to continue on the Crusher Trail.

0.7 Arrive at the impressive stone and steel iron ore crusher. Behind the crusher you will see a small trail heading up the hillside. Climb that trail and in a few yards come to a dirt road where you will view one of the Ruffner iron mines on the other side. When done, retrace your steps back to the crusher and continue on the Crusher Trail to the north. In less than 0.1 mile you'll return to the start of the short loop that led you to the crusher. Turn right here to head back to the Quarry Trail.

0.8 Pass an old, moss-covered stone foundation on your right.

1.0 Arrive once again at the intersection with the Ridge and Valley Trails. Don't turn onto the orange-blazed trail. Continue straight to the west.

1.1 Pass a stone wall on the right.

1.2 Arrive back at the Quarry Trail and turn left (southwest) onto the trail. In less than 0.1 mile you'll arrive at the Jimmie Dell / Winter Overlook Trail on the right (best viewed in winter). When done viewing, return to the Quarry Trail and turn right (southwest) to continue.

1.5 Come to a Y. The Quarry Trail continues to the south using the left fork. You'll return to this intersection later. Right now, take the right fork to the southwest onto the green-blazed Silent Journey Trail.

1.8 Come to a major intersection with the Silent Journey, Quarry, and Possum Loop. There is a kiosk with a map here and a wooden directional sign. Turn to the right (west) onto the yellow-blazed Possum Trail.

1.9 The Quarry Entrance Trail is to the left. Continue straight on the Possum Trail. You will start getting some views to your right of the surrounding hills and in a little bit Birmingham through the trees. In less than 0.1 mile you will pass the second Quarry Entrance Trail. Keep going straight to the northwest on the Possum Trail.

2.5 Arrive at Kudzu Corner.

2.6 Pass a very deep 10-foot by 10-foot stone and cement walled pit. It is extremely dangerous if you fall in.

2.7 Pass a bench on your left. In less than 0.1 mile come to an intersection with a sign showing directions for the

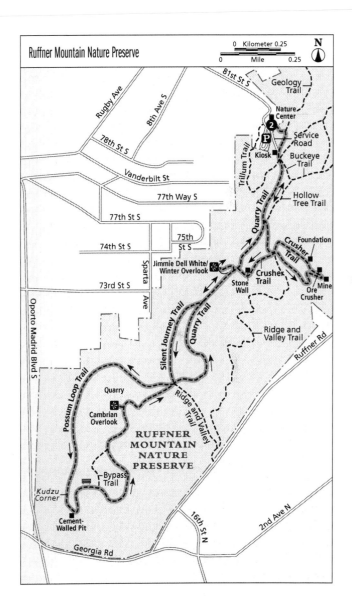

Bypass Trail (to the left), the Quarry Entrance (back the way you came), and the Possum Trail straight ahead. The Bypass Trail is a steep climb up a ridge where it rejoins the Possum Trail at mile 3.0. Continue straight to the east on the Possum Trail.

2.8 Pass another cement foundation on the right.

3.0 Come to a Y and the upper intersection with the Bypass Trail on the left fork. A sign here shows directions. Take the right fork to the north to continue on the Possum Trail.

3.2 Come to a side trail on the left for a splendid view of the quarry from above. When done viewing retrace your steps and turn left (north) to continue on the Possum Trail.

3.3 Another side trail on the left with stone stairs going up a small hill takes you to the Cambrian Overlook for yet another relaxing view of the quarry. When done, retrace your steps to the main trail. There is a Y here. Take the right fork to the southeast to stay on the Possum Trail.

3.5 Arrive back at the intersection from mile 1.8. Take the right fork to the east and follow the white-blazed Quarry Trail.

4.6 Arrive back at the trailhead.

3 Moss Rock Preserve

A world of incredible natural beauty awaits you at Moss Rock Preserve, a unique city park located in the town of Hoover. The preserve is a green space filled with amazing rock formations and a good smattering of waterfalls.

Start: Sulphur Springs trailhead
Distance: 4.9-mile out-and-back with center loop
Hiking time: About 2.5 hours
Difficulty: Easy to moderate
Trail surface: Dirt and rock
Best season: Year-round
Other trail users: None
Canine compatibility: Dogs permitted; leash required
Land status: City preserve

Schedule: Year-round; sunrise to sunset
Fees and permits: None
Maps: USGS Helena, AL; trail map available online at City of Hoover website
Contact: City of Hoover Parks Dept., 5500 Stadium Trace Pkwy., Hoover 35244; (205) 739-7141; www.hooveral.org/index.aspx?NID=219

Finding the trailhead: From I-459 exit 10, head northwest on John Hawkins Parkway. Travel 0.2 mile and turn right onto Grove Boulevard. Travel 0.6 mile and turn left onto Preserve Parkway. Travel 1 mile and turn left onto Sulphur Springs Road. The well-marked trailhead is 0.1 mile ahead on the right. **Trailhead GPS:** N33 22.586' / W86 51.204'

The Hike

This is truly an oasis in the midst of a bustling residential area. Driving through a nice subdivision with neatly manicured lawns and small shops lining the roadways, it's hard to believe that such an area exists, but there it is. You are suddenly removed from the busy town and immersed in a beautiful, natural wonderland.

The 349-acre Moss Rock Preserve is laced with 12 miles of hiking trails that can be used to create loop hikes of various lengths and difficulties. Along these trails you will pass unique geologic formations like Turtle Rock and Hole in Rock plus an ancient Native American rock shelter. Throughout the preserve, beautiful, shimmering creeks tumble down the hillside to fill the wide Hurricane Branch, creating sparkling cascading waterfalls on their way.

Moss Rock is also a plant lover's paradise. Within its borders, 66 species of trees will be found including longleaf pine and natural bonsai. You will also find 136 species of wildflowers including spiderwort, bird's-foot violet, bellwort, and liverleaf growing trailside and on rock outcroppings. Many rare species can be found at one of only thirty-five sandstone glades in the world. If you find yourself at the glade and off the trail for some reason, please use caution and only walk on the rock and avoid stepping on any plants.

This 4.9-mile out-and-back with a loop in the middle gives you a good sampling of everything there is to see at Moss Rock. It begins at the Sulphur Springs trailhead and uses trails named after the color they were blazed.

Keep in mind that waterfalls in Alabama are seasonal and may or may not be flowing in the heat of summer. The best time to visit to see the falls of the preserve is in fall or spring.

The trails at Moss Rock are well maintained so you won't have any trouble finding your way and are well marked with signage at intersections.

Miles and Directions

0.0 Start at the trailhead on the east side of the parking lot. In less than 0.1 mile, the trail turns right onto the Blue Trail.

0.1 Arrive at Patriotic Junction where the Red, White, and Blue Trails intersect. Turn left (east) onto the White Trail.

0.4 Pass a bench on the left.

0.5 Cross a seasonal creek and in 100 feet cross it again.

0.8 Pass Lower Tunnel Falls on the right. Continue straight to the north and cross the creek over a bridge to the east. Upper Tunnel Falls will be on your left as you cross.

0.9 The Red Trail comes in on the right (south) at Sign #4. Continue straight (east) on the White Trail. Cross a bridge over Hurricane Creek. There is a small cascade on the left.

1.1 Cross the creek once again over a bridge to the north. Turn right and in a few yards you will come to Lower Falls. When done viewing, return to the bridge but do not cross it. Instead, head north on the Blue Trail to Upper Falls.

1.2 Arrive at the Sandstone Glade. The trail continues to the north.

1.4 Pass a small seasonal cascade to the right. In less than 0.1 mile, arrive at Upper Falls. Topping out on the ridge, turn right (northeast) to continue on the Blue Trail. In less than 0.1 mile, pass a large boulder with a small rock shelter.

1.7 Cross a small creek and just after, turn left (northwest) on a side trail and in less than 0.1 mile, arrive at a small waterfall on the left. When ready, turn around and retrace your steps to the Blue Trail.

1.8 Back on the Blue Trail turn left (northeast).

1.9 Arrive at Turtle Rock. Turn right (southeast) here to rejoin the White Trail.

2.1 Cross a bridge over Hurricane Creek, then turn left (east) onto the Orange Trail.

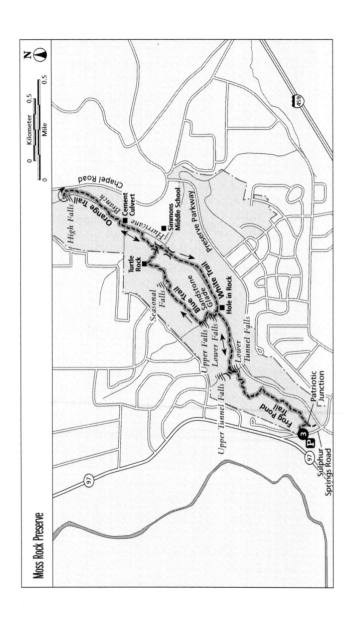

Moss Rock Preserve

High Falls

Chapel Road

Orange Trail

Cement
Culvert

Hurricane Branch

Simmons
Middle School

Preserve Parkway

Turtle
Rock

Seasonal
Falls

Blue Trail

Sandstone
Glade

White Trail

Hole in Rock

Upper Falls

Lower Falls

Lower
Tunnel Falls

Upper Tunnel Falls

Frog Pond Trail

Patriotic
Junction

97

Sulphur
Springs Road

P 3

459

N

0   0.5
Kilometer

0   0.5
Mile

2.2 Come to sign #9 at a Y. Turn left (northeast). Do a little rock hopping and pick your way across the creek, picking up the Orange Trail on the opposite side. Once across, the trail makes a sharp left turn.

2.3 Pass a cement culvert on the right for runoff. You will be following alongside a rocky creek and will have some boulders to scamper over.

2.4 Continue straight (northeast) on the Orange Trail, crossing under a powerline.

2.5 There is a subtle Y in the trail. Straight ahead it is very rutted. Take the left fork.

2.6 Scramble up some rocks next to the creek.

2.7 Arrive at High Falls. When finished exploring, turn around and retrace your steps to the bridge at mile 2.1.

3.3 Back at the bridge, cross Hurricane Creek once again, then turn left onto the White Trail.

3.6 Cross a small seasonal feeder creek, then pass sign #7. In less than 0.1 mile, cross a stream to the southwest.

3.8 Arrive at Hole in Rock. Continue straight to the southwest on the White Trail, passing the bridge you crossed at mile 1.1. You will now be retracing your steps back to the trailhead.

4.2 Cross the bridge at Tunnel Falls once again.

4.8 The trail to the Frog Pond heads off to the left (south). If you choose, you could take this short trail, which will return you to the White Trail in 0.1 mile. For this description, continue straight (southwest) on the White Trail.

4.9 Arrive back at the trailhead.

4 **Ruffner Mountain Wetlands**

Explore the natural side of Ruffner Mountain on this hike to a beautiful pond and wetland. The route uses an old, crushed-gravel railroad bed of the Birmingham Mineral Railroad Line that once delivered iron ore to nearby foundries before ducking into the woods to circle a pond where any number of waterfowl may be seen.

Start: Trailhead on Ruffner Road
Distance: 2.0-mile out-and-back
Hiking time: About 1 hour
Difficulty: Easy
Trail surface: Dirt and gravel road, dirt and rock footpath
Best season: Year-round
Other trail users: None
Canine compatibility: Leashed dogs permitted
Land status: Nonprofit nature center
Schedule: Sunrise to sunset
Fees and permits: Parking fee. Pay for this by either using the QR code on the sign at the trailhead with your cell phone or drop the money in the donation box on the opposite side of the gate. An alternative, and one that helps the preserve continue its mission, is to become a member, which includes a yearly parking pass. See the website under Contact.
Maps: USGS Irondale, AL; trail maps available at trailhead kiosk
Contact: Ruffner Mountain Nature Center, 1214 81st St., Birmingham 35206; (205) 833-8264; www.ruffnermountain.org

Finding the trailhead: From the intersection of I-65 and US 11 / 1st Avenue North, take US 11 / 1st Avenue Northwest 4.6 miles. Turn right onto 57th Street North. In less than 0.1 mile, turn left onto 1st Avenue South. In less than 0.1 mile, make a slight right onto Georgia Road and travel 2 miles. Turn left onto Ruffner Road and travel 2 miles. Parking and the trailhead will be on the left. **Trailhead GPS:** N33 33.521' / W86 41.338'

The Hike

The Ruffner Mountain Nature Preserve hike explores the mining history of Ruffner Mountain. This hike will take you along an eastern ridge of the mountain to view a beautiful pond and wetland.

This 2-mile out-and-back uses a combination of an old, crushed-gravel jeep road and the bed of the old Birmingham Mineral Railroad (BMRR) plus a nice, narrow dirt footpath to reach the wetland. The BMRR section is part of the same path in Red Mountain Park that once hauled iron ore via railcar to the area's foundries. In fact, all along the route you will see evidence of its mining and railroad past—hand-built stone culverts, old stone and brick structures left for nature to reclaim, even a large steel water valve that is left open, shooting water into the pond like a runaway fire hydrant.

This hike to Ruffner's wetlands is a birders' paradise and is part of the Alabama Birding Trail. Along the route you may see a variety of tangers, warblers, and thrushes as well as pileated and hairy woodpeckers, eastern towhees, catbirds, and yellow throats, to name only a few.

The hike is an easy walker, one that the entire family can enjoy.

Miles and Directions

0.0 Start at the gate on Ruffner Road. At this point, the trail is a wide, gravel jeep road.

0.2 Pass a pond to the left.

0.3 Come to an intersection. A sign points the way to the nature center (straight ahead). Turn left (southwest) onto Lizard Loop. You are now hiking on a portion of the old BMRR railroad.

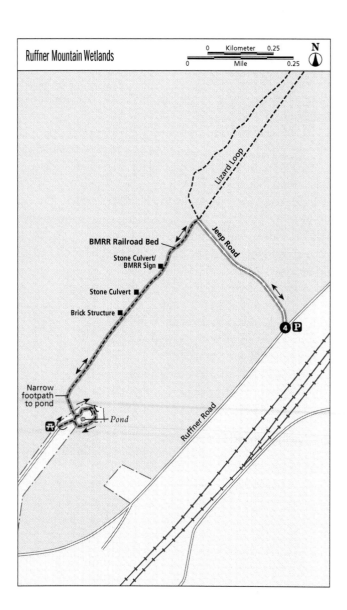

Ruffner Mountain Wetlands

0 Kilometer 0.25
0 Mile 0.25

N

Lizard Loop

BMRR Railroad Bed

Jeep Road

Stone Culvert/
BMRR Sign ■

Stone Culvert ■

Brick Structure ■

4 P

Narrow
footpath
to pond

Pond

Ruffner Road

0.5 Pass the first of several stone culverts off to the side of the trail and a BMRR sign.

0.7 Pass another culvert and BMRR sign.

0.9 Turn left onto a narrow dirt footpath. In less than 0.1 mile, pass an old steel railroad water valve that is open and gushing water. A few yards later, cross under a powerline and turn left onto another narrow dirt footpath to begin the loop around the pond and wetland.

1.0 A narrow strip of land bisects the pond. A wooden boardwalk used to be here. Now, cross to the other side of the pond over the land bridge. On the other side, turn right to continue around the pond.

1.1 Turn left onto a side trail to make a stop at the picnic pavilion at the wetland to enjoy the silence and nature. When ready, turn around then retrace your steps to the trailhead.

2.0 Arrive back at the trailhead.

5 Boulder Canyon Nature Trail

This short but beautiful little hike in Vestavia Hills is teeming with cascades that tumble down short rock bluffs and rocky boulder-strewn channels, hence the name Boulder Canyon. The waterfalls and cascades range from short 3-foot drops to a couple 6-foot cascades and the grand finale, a 15-foot plunge at the end of the hike.

Start: At the trailhead to the north of the parking lot through a wooden fence

Distance: 1.0-mile loop

Hiking time: About 1 hour

Difficulty: Easy

Trail surface: Narrow dirt and rock footpath

Best season: Sept through Apr

Other trail users: None

Canine compatibility: Dogs permitted; leash required

Land Status: City school property / city park

Schedule: Open sunrise to sunset

Fees and permits: None

Maps: USGS Birmingham South, Alabama

Contact: Vestavia Hills Parks and Recreation, 1289 Montgomery Hwy., Vestavia Hills 35216; (205) 978-0166; www.vhal.org/departments/parks-recreation/facilities

Special considerations: Do not hike the trail while school is in session

Finding the trailhead: From Birmingham start at the intersection of I-20 and I-65. Take I-65 south 8.2 miles. Take exit 252 (US 31) and turn left onto US 31 North. Take US 31 North 1.3 miles and turn right onto Vestridge Drive. Travel 0.2 mile and continue straight on Badham Drive. Travel 0.4 mile and turn left onto Willoughby Road. In less than 0.1 mile, turn left onto Merry Fox Lane. The parking lot and trailhead will be on the left in 0.1 mile. **Trailhead GPS:** N33 25.708' / W86 47.183'

The Hike

This 1-mile loop hike begins to the north across the street from the parking lot on Merry Fox Lane. The trails meander around the property, interconnecting to give you nice views of several drops and cascades including one beautiful long cascade that tumbles over its boulder-strewn channel for some 200 feet from end to end. The hike culminates with the main waterfall—a 15-foot plunge near the school.

While there really isn't a right or wrong way to hike Boulder Canyon, the route isn't blazed, so you need to keep your head up and an eye out for the path. The hike is suitable for older children, but if you have young children, there are some very narrow sections with pretty steep drops. You may want to consider doing a shorter 0.6-mile out-and-back by reversing the directions here, starting at the end of the hike, passing the main waterfall near the school before visiting the long cascade at mile 0.7 in the description where you will turn around and head back to the parking area.

The trail is a dirt and rock-strewn path with a few short climbs up and down hills using 6-by-6 railroad-tie stairs. These stairs have rope handrails next to them to help you down. The ties are held in place with rebar and in some cases, those steel bars stick up an inch or two above the wood. Watch your step so you don't trip or step on them.

Miles and Directions

0.0 Start at the trailhead across the street from the parking lot to the north. In less than 0.1 mile, come to a Y with a tree in the middle of the fork. Take the right fork to the northeast.

0.2 Come to an intersection. Continue straight to the northwest. In less than 0.1 mile, pass a bench on the left and head

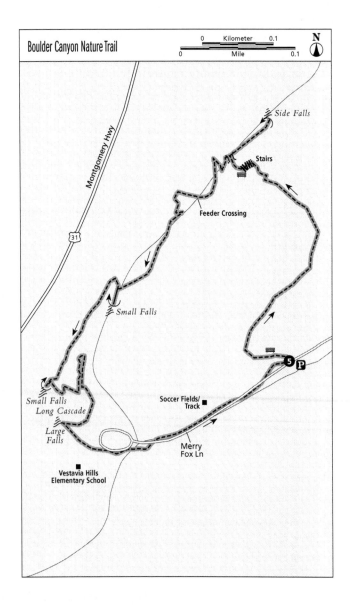

Boulder Canyon Nature Trail

Side Falls

Stairs

Feeder Crossing

Small Falls

*Small Falls
Long Cascade*

*Large
Falls*

Vestavia Hills
Elementary School

Soccer Fields/
Track

Merry
Fox Ln

Montgomery Hwy

31

5 P

Kilometer
Mile

0   0.1

N

steeply downhill toward the creek using 6-by-6 railroad-tie stairs.

0.3 Come to the creek and a bridge. A short side trail on each side of the bridge invites you to turn right and head upstream 100 feet to explore the first falls. When ready, cross the bridge and head left (southwest).

0.4 Come to a Y. Take the right fork to the northwest and come to the second tiered falls. Cross the stream over the rocky bed of the feeder to the west where it then turns left and returns to follow the creek to the north.

0.5 View another small waterfall on the left.

0.7 A nondescript trail comes in from the right. Take the trail down the 6-by-6 steps to the falls below. You will be in the middle of the long cascade. When ready, head back up the stairs and turn right (southeast) to continue on the trail.

0.8 Take the short side trail to the right (west) that leads you to the main waterfall. When ready, turn left and head southeast toward the school.

0.9 Cross a wooden footbridge to the cul-de-sac of the school parking lot. Follow Merry Fox Lane to the east, passing a playground and soccer field on your left.

1.0 Arrive back at the trailhead.

6 Turkey Creek Nature Preserve

A fun walk in the woods awaits you at the Turkey Creek Nature Preserve in Pinson. This loop hike takes you to the top of a ridgeline then down to the banks of the fast-flowing waters of Turkey Creek itself and to a rushing cascade that is the perfect summertime swimming hole.

Start: From the trailhead on Narrows Road

Distance: 2.3-mile loop

Hiking time: About 2 hours

Difficulty: Easy

Trail Surface: Dirt footpath, paved footpath and road

Best seasons: Year-round

Other Trail Users: None

Canine Compatibility: Leashed dogs permitted

Land Status: City park, Alabama Forever Wild tract

Schedule: Dawn to dusk

Fees and Permits: None

Maps: USGS Pinson, Alabama

Contact: Turkey Creek Nature Preserve, 3906 Turkey Creek Blvd., Pinson 35126; (205) 680-4116; www.turkeycreeknp.com/

Finding the trailhead: From Birmingham on I-59 exit 128 take AL 79 North for 10.4 miles. Turn left onto CR 131 / Narrows Road. In 0.2 mile turn right onto Turkey Creek Road and follow it 0.7 mile. The trailhead will be on the left. Remember that this is a one-way loop road. **Trailhead GPS:** N33 42.171' / W86 41.781'

The Hike

Turkey Creek Nature Preserve is the perfect example of conservation at its finest with a state agency partnering with the city, nonprofits, and a college to protect what has been described as one of the most biologically diverse habitats in the region.

The mission of this partnership is primarily to protect the preserve's namesake, the rushing waters of Turkey Creek, which is the home of several rare and endangered species of fish including the watercress darter, rush darter, and the vermilion darter. The vermilion darter is found only here in Turkey Creek and nowhere else in the world.

If you are into birding, you've come to the right place. According to Alabama Birding Trails, the number of birds you can add to your list is tremendous. Some species include eastern Phoebes, great blue herons, red tail and broad wing hawks, Acadian flycatchers, and a lengthy list of warblers to name only a few.

This hike takes in two different sides of the preserve. It begins by climbing a ridge and following it for a short distance where you will have a couple of views of the surrounding hillsides (the best time is in the winter when the foliage is little to none). It then drops down to the swift-flowing creek itself that is lined with impressive boulders and outcroppings creating many rapids and waterfalls. Be sure to bring a swimsuit. The pool formed at the bottom of these cascades is a glorious swimming hole. There are changing rooms located at the trailhead.

You will be using two trails and a bit of a road walk to complete the loop—the blue-blazed Thompson Trace Trail and the Highlands Trail. Be sure to carve out some time during your visit to explore the three other trails in the preserve—the Narrows Ridge (which is also a mountain bike trail), the Hanby Hollow Trail, and the Boy Scout Trail. They interconnect with one another allowing you to form different loops.

The road walk portion of this hike is only 0.4 mile in length but has some really nice views of the rapids in the creek. The best view of the trip, however, comes just at the end when you get to walk through a boulder field next to a wide set of rapids and falls.

Miles and Directions

0.0   Start at the parking lot trailhead. The trail begins on the northeast side of the parking lot. It is a short scramble up a 10-foot clay bank. The trail is a dirt footpath with blue blazes; sometimes yellow diamond markers with either a hiker or an arrow will be used.

0.4   Through the trees you can glimpse the rapids to the northwest.

0.5   Reach the top of the ridge. The path levels out here. A view of the valley can be seen to the southeast.

0.7   Come to a rock outcropping on the left (southeast). A 30-foot side trail takes you to the edge.

1.0   Begin a steep downhill walk. Narrows Road can be seen on your left (south).

1.1   Reach the bottom of the incline, cross an intermittent creek, and start a climb up the other side.

1.4   Come out of the woods and turn right onto the paved Turkey Creek Road. A picnic area will be on your left (west).

1.5   Cross the road to the northwest. This is the beginning of the Highland Trail (there is a sign here). Cross through four yellow posts, positioned to keep vehicles off the path, and begin a moderate climb up the hill.

1.8   Following a steep downhill, arrive once again at Narrows Road. Turn left (east) onto the road. Turkey Creek will soon be seen on the left (north).

1.9   You will start getting your first good look at the rapids of Turkey Creek to the left (northeast).

Turkey Creek Nature Preserve

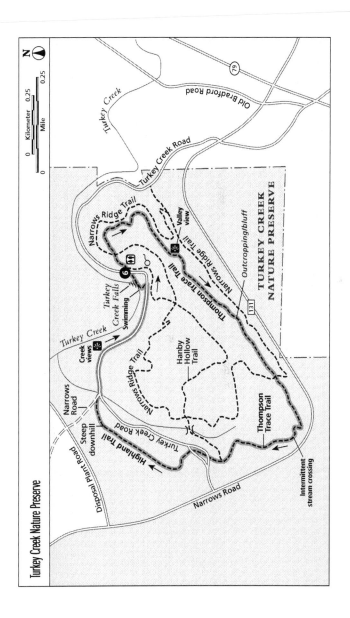

2.1 Pass a beautiful 30- to 50-foot wide rapid in the creek and a view of an upcoming waterfall.

2.2 Arrive at the waterfall. There are a few impressive large boulders here. Turn left (northwest) off the road and head down toward the boulder and creek (there is a picnic table here). Follow the creek less than 0.1 mile to the northwest then northeast and you will come to a set of stairs that leads back to Narrows Road. At the top of the stairs cross the road to the northeast.

2.3 Arrive back at the trailhead / parking lot.

7 King's Chair Loop

Travel to the popular Oak Mountain State Park to hike the most challenging of treks we will tackle to take in the breathtaking views from the King's Chair Overlook.

Start: North Trailhead on Oak Mountain Park Road
Distance: 4.2-mile loop
Hiking time: About 3 hours
Difficulty: Moderate to difficult
Trail surface: Dirt and rock
Best season: Winter through late spring
Other trail users: Cyclists on White and Red Trails
Canine compatibility: Leashed dogs permitted

Land status: State park
Schedule: Sunrise to sunset
Fess and permits: Day-use fee
Maps: USGS Chelsea, AL; trail maps available at entrance gate or camp store
Contact: Oak Mountain State Park, 200 Terrace Dr., Pelham 35124; (205) 620-2520; www.alapark.com/parks/oak-mountain-state-park

Finding the trailhead: From Pelham on I-65 at exit 248, take AL 119 South / Cahaba Valley Road 0.2 mile and turn left onto Oak Mountain Road. Travel 1.9 miles and turn left onto John Findley III Drive. In 0.3 mile you will arrive at the park entrance gate, where you pay your day-use fee. Continue straight (northeast) 5.8 miles on John Findley III Road. Watch for the many cyclists on the road. The trailhead is on the right side of the road and well marked. Parking is on the left.
Trailhead GPS: N33 21.453' / W86 42.285'

The Hike

Next to Peavine Falls, the most popular destination at Oak Mountain State Park, is the King's Chair Overlook, but you will have to work to get there.

The "chair" is a tall rock bluff that offers those who venture to it an incredible, breathtaking view of the Pelham Mountains, valleys, and Belcher Lake. The drawback—the climb to get there. The hike has a 734-foot elevation gain.

We will use four trails to make the loop: Blue Trail (South Rim Trail), King's Chair Overlook Trail, Red-Blue Connector South, and Red Trail (Double Oak Trail). The trails are dirt and rock strewn and, like all trails in the park, are well blazed with markers in the color of the trail name (blue markers for the Blue Trail, etc.), and intersections are obvious with wooden markers directing you. There are also mile markers that you can use to establish your location if you call park rangers in case of emergency.

The hike begins at the north trailhead on John Findley III Drive, the "hub" of hiking and biking trails where several trails begin. There is a restroom here and changing rooms. The Blue Trail (also known as the South Rim Trail) begins across the road from the parking area and starts off quite easy, but don't get a false sense that this will be a breeze. The hike up the mountain is a steady climb.

Miles and Directions doesn't cover this, but at 1.0 mile into the hike, you will pass the Eagle's Nest Overlook Trail on the left. If you choose, you can deviate from the route described here to take this 0.2-mile trail to a second overlook. The trail rejoins the route described in the Miles and Directions at mile 1.4.

If you'd like to spend a night, there is a primitive campsite located just below the chair. You must reserve the site through the park office (see Contact).

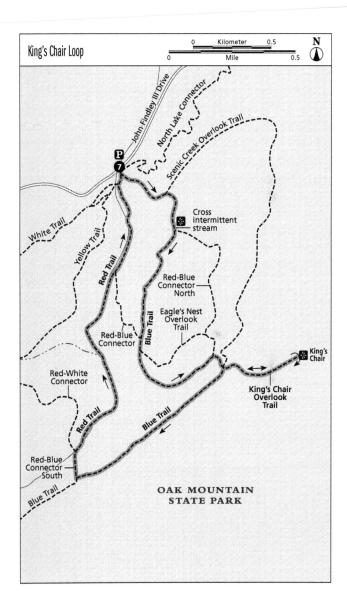

King's Chair Loop

Kilometer 0.5

Mile 0.5

N

John Findley III Drive

North Lake Connector

Scenic Creek Overlook Trail

P
7

Cross intermittent stream

White Trail

Yellow Trail

Red Trail

Red-Blue Connector North

Eagle's Nest Overlook Trail

Red-Blue Connector

Red-White Connector

King's Chair

King's Chair Overlook Trail

Red Trail

Blue Trail

Blue Trail

Red-Blue Connector South

Blue Trail

OAK MOUNTAIN STATE PARK

Miles and Directions

0.0 Start from the parking lot and cross the road to reach the North Trailhead (there are obvious signs here). On the other side, go straight to the south and pick up the blue blazes of the Blue Trail.

0.2 Pass the Scenic Creek Overlook Trail on the left.

0.4 Cross a seasonal creek. There is a small overlook here.

0.9 Pass the east end of the Red-Blue Connector North trail.

1.0 Pass the west end of the Eagle's Nest Overlook Trail on the left.

1.4 Pass the east end of the Eagle's Nest Overlook Trail on the left. In less than 0.1 mile, take the left fork onto the King's Chair Overlook Trail.

1.8 Arrive at the King's Chair Overlook. Enjoy the view. When ready, turn around and retrace your steps back to the Blue Trail.

2.1 Arrive back at the intersection from mile 1.4 and turn left (southwest) onto the Blue Trail.

2.9 The Blue Trail continues straight to the southwest. Turn right here (north) onto the Red-Blue Connector South trail.

3.0 Turn right (northeast) onto the Red Trail.

3.3 Pass the Yellow-Blue Connector trail on the left.

3.8 Pass the west end of the Red-Blue Connector North trail on the right.

4.1 The White and Yellow Trails merge from the left. Continue straight to the north.

4.2 The Blue Trail rejoins the Red, White, and Yellow Trails. In less than 0.1 mile, arrive back at the trailhead.

8 Maggie's Glen Loop

This hike to Maggie's Glen at Oak Mountain features a nice walk alongside a sparkling—but seasonal—stream and the glen itself that is located within a hollow, making it the perfect spot for picnicking, especially in the spring with the stream cascading next to the trail and white beeches and dogwoods flowering around you.

Start: North Trailhead on Oak Mountain Park Road
Distance: 2.2-mile lollipop
Hiking time: About 2 hours
Difficulty: Easy
Trail surface: Dirt and rock
Best season: Winter to late spring
Other trail users: Cyclists
Canine compatibility: Leashed dogs permitted

Land status: State park
Schedule: Sunrise to sunset
Fess and permits: Day-use fee
Maps: USGS Chelsea, AL; trail maps available at entrance gate or camp store
Contact: Oak Mountain State Park, 200 Terrace Dr., Pelham 35124; (205) 620-2520; www.alapark.com/parks/oak-mountain-state-park

Finding the trailhead: From Pelham on I-65 at exit 248, take AL 119 South / Cahaba Valley Road 0.2 mile and turn left onto Oak Mountain Road. Travel 1.9 miles and turn left onto John Findley III Drive. In 0.3 mile you will arrive at the park entrance gate, where you pay your day-use fee. Continue straight (northeast) 5.8 miles on John Findley III Road. Watch for the many cyclists on the road. The trailhead is on the right side of the road and well marked. Parking is on the left.
Trailhead GPS: N33 21.453' / W86 42.285'

The Hike

This beautiful little 2.2-mile loop hike is a fun and relaxing walk in the woods for the entire family. The hike uses a combination of three trails at Oak Mountain State Park—the Red, the White, and the Yellow—that follows alongside a nice stream flowing down from a hollow, tumbling down a rocky bed with several small cascades. Short side trails along the route take you to its banks for a better view or to dip your feet in the cold mountain stream.

This hike to Maggie's Glen is especially beautiful in early spring when the flowering dogwoods and white beeches bloom and in fall when the hardwoods are ablaze with fiery color.

The trail's namesake, Maggie's Glen, is at the halfway point of the hike. Here, you will find several benches courtesy of local Eagle Scouts and easy access to the stream. Pack a lunch and spend some time here. It is the perfect place to let the cares of the world slip away as you sit and take in the soothing sounds of the rushing water. If you have kids, it's a wonderful place for them to run around and enjoy the forest.

There is an informational kiosk here that provides plenty of information about the local wildlife.

The trails are blazed with colored reflective markers painted the same color as the trail name—white, yellow, or red. Along the route you will notice 4-by-4 posts with numbers on them corresponding to mileages on the trail, like mile markers along the highway. If you get lost or find yourself in trouble, you can call the park ranger and tell them what trail you are on and what marker you are near.

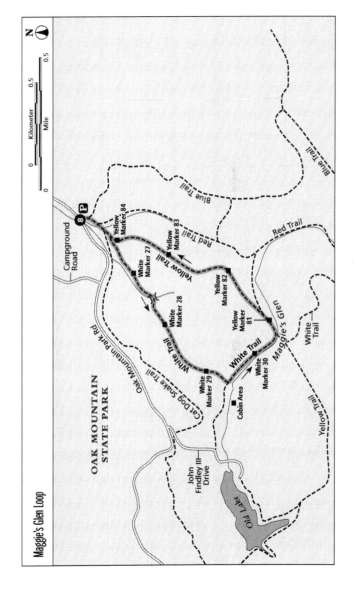

Miles and Directions

0.0 Start from the parking lot and cross the road to reach the North Trailhead (there are obvious signs here). On the other side, go straight to the south. The trail starts as a 10-foot-wide gravel path and is actually three trails: the Red, the White, and the Yellow.

0.1 Take the right fork at a Y (a sign shows that this is the way to Maggie's Glen), crossing a runoff ditch over a short foot-bridge. The trail is now a narrow dirt footpath. Come to a Y. The left fork is your return trip on the Yellow Trail. Take the right fork toward the west on the White Trail.

0.4 Pass white mile marker 27, then cross a stream over a 15-foot bridge.

0.5 You will be walking next to a creek on the right and will cross it over a footbridge in a few feet.

0.9 Come to a fork. A sign here points the way to cabins to the north (back the way you came) and Maggie's Glen to the left. Take the left fork.

1.0 The trail begins to parallel a wide stream on the right with nice cascades.

1.1 Pass a short side trail to the stream on the right (nice cascades here). Pass white marker 30 and in 50 feet pass another side trail to the stream.

1.2 Come to a sign indicating the direction of the White Trail. There is a rock jumble and cascades to the right. In 200 feet you will arrive at Maggie's Glen. There is an informational kiosk and four benches here, along with a three-prong fork in the trail: the Red-Yellow Connector (center), the Yellow Trail (left), and the White/Yellow Trail (right, to the south, with a bridge crossing the stream). Take the left fork uphill on the Yellow Trail.

1.3 Pass yellow marker 81. This is a climb to the top of a ridge on the uphill side of the Maggie's Glen stream (which is now on your right). You will see nice views along this ridge in the winter.

2.1 Pass yellow marker 84. In 100 feet you will be back at the intersection with the White Trail at mile 0.2. Turn right onto the White/Yellow Trail and retrace your steps to the trailhead.

2.2 Arrive back at the trailhead.

9 Treetop Trail / Alabama Wildlife Center

This fun, easy hike for grownups and kids alike starts along the banks of a cascading brook then follows a long boardwalk past spacious enclosures where live birds that cannot be returned to the wild because of their condition are cared for. The hike culminates in a visit to the Alabama Wildlife Center where sick or injured birds and animals are rehabbed so they can be released.

Start: At the day-use parking lot on Terrace Drive
Distance: 1.1-mile out-and-back
Hiking time: About 1 hour (leave time for a visit to the Animal Rehab Center)
Difficulty: Easy
Trail surface: Dirt footpath, boardwalk
Best season: Year-round
Other trail users: None
Canine compatibility: Leashed dogs permitted
Land status: State park

Schedule: Trail: sunrise to sunset; rehabilitation center: daily 9 a.m. to 5 p.m.
Fess and permits: Day-use fee
Maps: USGS Chelsea, AL; USGS Helena, AL; trail maps available at entrance gate or camp store
Contact: Oak Mountain State Park, 200 Terrace Dr., Pelham 35124; (205) 620-2520; www.alapark.com/parks/oak-mountain-state-park; Alabama Wildlife Center, www.alabamawildlifecenter.org

Finding the trailhead: From Pelham take I-65 exit 246 and turn right onto AL 119 South/Cahaba Valley Road. In less than 0.1 mile, turn left onto Oak Mountain Park Road / State Park Road. Travel 1.9 miles and turn left onto John Findley III Drive. Travel 2.6 miles and make a right turn onto Terrace Drive. Travel 1 mile and park in the day-use parking lot. The trailhead is across the street from the parking area to the southwest. **Trailhead GPS:** N33 19.501' / W86 45.447'

The Hike

Oak Mountain State Park plays host to the Alabama Wildlife Center (AWC), the state's oldest and largest wildlife rehabilitation facility. Since its inception in 1990, the center has cared for over 2,000 wild birds in need of medical attention including over 100 different species. When deemed healthy enough, the birds are released back into the wild.

Now, some of the birds cannot survive on their own in the wild, so AWC provides a special home for them—spacious, natural enclosures that you will see along the Treetop Trail.

This portion of the trail is an elevated boardwalk that leads you past the enclosures, each with an informative sign telling you about the birds, including several owls such as barred, screech, and great horned as well as turkey vultures and red tail hawks. Many times a volunteer from the center will be on hand to answer questions.

For most of the hike on the dirt footpath portion, you will be walking next to a beautiful, little cascading brook. This is a seasonal stream so it may not be flowing in the heat of summer.

The trail finally narrows as it heads up a dirt footpath until it reaches the top of a ridge and the AWC facility itself. Inside is an amazing display of educational exhibits as well as live birds. You may see hummingbirds and butterflies in their garden or watch as the volunteers feed orphaned babies. There is also a large open building where rehabilitating red tail hawks can stretch their wings and freely fly out.

Be sure to visit the AWC website (see Contact) for special educational programs put on by volunteers.

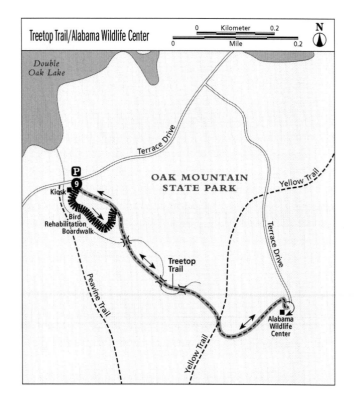

Treetop Trail/Alabama Wildlife Center

0   Kilometer   0.2
0   Mile   0.2

N

Double Oak Lake

Terrace Drive

OAK MOUNTAIN STATE PARK

Yellow Trail

P
9

Kiosk

Bird Rehabilitation Boardwalk

Terrace Drive

Treetop Trail

Peavine Trail

Alabama Wildlife Center

Yellow Trail

Miles and Directions

0.0   Start from the trailhead across the street to the south from the day-use parking area on Terrace Drive. A large wooden sign and a short footbridge over a ditch mark the way. Just after the bridge there is a Y. A kiosk here describes the trail. Take the right fork and head up the stairs and boardwalk to view birds that cannot be released to the wild because of their condition.

0.2   Come off the boardwalk at a wide dirt footpath that heads to the left and right (northwest/southeast). Turn to the right (southeast) onto the Treetop Trail. A really nice little creek flows alongside the trail. In less than 0.1 mile you will cross the creek over a short footbridge.

0.3   Cross the creek again over a footbridge and make a short climb uphill over some rock stairs. In 100 feet cross the creek again over a footbridge.

0.4   The Yellow Trail enters from the left (north). Continue straight (southeast). In 100 feet come to a sign that shows the Yellow and Treetop Trails turning right (southwest). Do not turn here but continue straight to the south. The trail turns into a hard-packed trail bed. You will be walking between several buildings on each side of the trail on top of hills.

0.6   Arrive at the Alabama Wildlife Center. Take your time to visit the exhibits, talk to the volunteers, and visit the birds. When done, retrace your steps back to the boardwalk at mile 0.2.

1.1   Back at the boardwalk, instead of heading back up the boardwalk, continue straight on the wide dirt footpath to the trailhead. In 100 yards arrive back at the trailhead.

10 Peavine Falls Loop

This is one of the more difficult trails you will navigate with a steep downhill climb into the gorge that culminates in a visit to Oak Mountain State Park's centerpiece, Peavine Falls, a 65-foot tumbling cascade. While it is a steep walk down (see the Miles and Directions section for a shorter, easier option), it is still a popular route most any time of the year, with its lush forest and, of course, the waterfall itself.

Start: Northwest side of Peavine Falls parking lot on the green Peavine Falls Trail
Distance: 1.8-mile loop
Hiking time: About 2 hours
Difficulty: Moderate to difficult
Trail surface: Dirt, rock, gravel road
Best season: Winter to late spring
Other trail users: Cyclists
Canine compatibility: Leashed dogs permitted
Land status: State park

Schedule: Sunrise to sunset
Fess and permits: Day-use fee
Maps: USGS Chelsea, AL; trail maps available at entrance gate or camp store
Contact: Oak Mountain State Park, 200 Terrace Dr., Pelham 35124; (205) 620-2520; www.alapark.com/parks/oak-mountain-state-park
Special considerations: Waterfalls are seasonal in Alabama and may not be flowing in the heat of summer.

Finding the trailhead: From Pelham on I-65 at exit 248, take AL 119 South / Cahaba Valley Road for 0.2 mile and turn left onto Oak Mountain Road. Travel 2.7 miles and turn right onto Peavine Falls Road. Follow the winding road 3 miles to the parking lot. Be careful on the winding turns and watch out for bicycles. The Green Trail trailhead is on the northwest side of the parking lot. **Trailhead GPS:** N33 18.159' / W86 45.749'

The Hike

Every weekend, the Peavine Falls parking lot is full as people flock to the 65-foot waterfall that cascades down its rock wall into a clear, cold, boulder-strewn pool. Your best bet to avoid the crowds is to visit during the week in the morning.

When arriving at the parking lot, you will notice two sets of kiosks—one on the east side where you will end this hike on the White Trail, the other on the northwest side where the Green Trail begins, and that's where you will start the hike.

You will be using six trails to complete the loop—the Green, Green-White Connector, White, Blue, Falls Loop, Falls Creek, and Peavine Falls Trails. The trails consist of a dirt and rock footpath for most of their length except for the last 0.4 mile back to the parking lot on the White Trail that is a wide dirt and gravel road.

You begin on the Green Trail with a steady climb to the top of a ridge where dogwoods bloom and songbirds serenade you in the spring and the live oaks and silver maples paint a brilliant picture in the fall. In the winter with the leaves down, you will catch a few views of the surrounding hills. In summer, a variety of thrushes and wrens dart through the brush, and throughout the year broad-winged and red-shouldered hawks soar overhead.

Once you get to the bottom of the gorge, you will be at the base of the falls. When it's running full, it's a spectacular sight and its roar echoes off the walls of the gorge. Remember, waterfalls in Alabama, including Peavine, are seasonal and may not be flowing in the heat of summer.

To complete the loop, you will have to get your feet wet or do some rock scrambling. Cross the stream and pick up the trail on the other side. Use extreme caution and use your best judgment! If the stream is running fast and full, don't chance it. Turn around and head back the way you came.

As mentioned, the walk into and out of the gorge is quite steep and may be too steep for smaller children and dogs. An optional shorter and a bit easier out-and-back route is described in the Miles and Directions section.

With the exception of the Falls Loop and Peavine Falls Trails that use white diamond-shaped markers to lead the way, all the other trails have plenty of blazes to help keep you on track.

Miles and Directions

0.0 Start at the Green Trail trailhead located on the northwest side of the parking lot.

0.1 Pass the Red Trail on the left.

0.4 Arrive at the top of the ridge and a short side trail on the right with an overlook.

0.6 Turn right (south) and head very steeply downhill on the Green-White Connector Trail.

0.8 Arrive at Peavine Branch. Turn right (southwest) onto the White Trail, which follows alongside the creek.

0.9 Cross a 30-foot-long footbridge over the creek and pick up the Blue Trail on the opposite side. When water is flowing, there is a nice 50-foot-long sliding cascade off to your right. In less than 0.1 mile, come to a Y in the trail. Take the left fork to the northeast to continue on the Blue Trail.

1.0 Turn right (south) onto the Falls Creek Trail and begin a serious downhill climb.

1.1 Arrive at the base of the falls. When done exploring, turn left (southeast) and follow the bank of the creek. This is the Falls Creek Loop Trail.

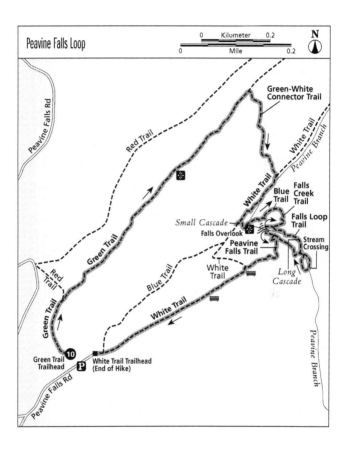

Peavine Falls Loop

Green-White
Connector Trail

Red Trail

White Trail

Peavine Falls Rd

Peavine Branch

Green Trail

White Trail

Blue
Trail

Falls
Creek
Trail

Falls Loop
Trail

Small Cascade

Falls Overlook

Stream
Crossing

Peavine Falls Trail

White
Trail

*Long
Cascade*

Red
Trail

Blue Trail

White Trail

Green Trail

Peavine Branch

10

Green Trail
Trailhead

P White Trail Trailhead
(End of Hike)

Peavine Falls Rd

0   Kilometer   0.2

0   Mile   0.2

N

1.2 Climb a set of stone stairs up a little hill. A really nice lower cascade begins here with a wide slide in the middle.

1.3 Pick your way carefully across the stream and pick up the loop trail on the other side.

1.4 Arrive once again at the base of the falls. Turn left (south) away from the stream and head steeply uphill to the south on the Peavine Falls Trail. In less than 0.1 mile, arrive at Falls Overlook. The trail switchbacks to the top of the ridge.

1.5 Top out on the rim of the gorge. Turn right (west) to continue on the Peavine Falls Trail. In less than 0.1 mile, arrive at the White Trail—a wide gravel road with benches on both sides. Head straight to the southwest on the White Trail.

1.6 Pass benches on both sides of the trail.

1.8 Arrive at the parking lot and the White Trail trailhead.

Option: For an easier trek that's a little less steep or if you can't ford the creek because it's too dangerous, do a 1.0-mile out-and-back by starting where the hike described here ends (the White Trail Trailhead) and reverse the above directions from mile 1.8 to mile 1.4 and the base of the falls. At the falls, simply turn around and retrace your steps back to the start.

11 Tannehill Ironworks Historical State Park

You will explore more of the iron and steel history of Birmingham on this loop hike around the Tannehill Ironworks Historical State Park. This loop will take you past the tremendous stone furnace that has been carefully reconstructed, past the rolling blue-green waters of Roupes Creek (aka Mud Creek), and the cemetery of the enslaved people who helped build and work the ironworks.

Start: Behind the Iron and Steel Museum of Alabama

Distance: 4.1-mile lollipop

Hiking time: About 2 hours

Difficulty: Easy

Trail surface: Dirt and gravel

Best season: Year-round

Other trail users: Cyclists

Canine compatibility: Dogs permitted; leash required

Land status: Alabama historical state park

Schedule: Sunrise to sunset; visitor center and museum: 10 a.m. to 4 p.m.

Fees and permits: Day-use fee; small fee for museum admission

Maps: USGS McCalla, AL; trail maps available at country store

Contact: Tannehill Ironworks Historical State Park, 12632 Confederate Pkwy., McCalla 35111; (205) 477-5711; www.tannehillstatepark.org

Finding the trailhead: From the intersection of I-459 and I-20 West / I-59 South, take I-20 West / I-59 South 5 miles. Take exit 100 (Abernant/Bucksville) and turn left onto AL 216 East. (Shortly after turning onto AL 216, it becomes Bucksville Road.) Follow AL 216 / Bucksville Road 0.6 mile and make a slight right onto Tannehill Parkway. Travel 1.9 miles and turn right onto Eastern Valley Road. In less than 0.1 mile, turn left onto Confederate Parkway. The park entrance is ahead in 0.7 mile. **Trailhead GPS:** N33 14.970' / W87 04.297'

The Hike

As you saw earlier in Red Mountain Park and Ruffner Mountain Nature Preserve, the city of Birmingham became the major city it is today because of its mining and steel industry. During its heyday, the city rivaled Pittsburgh in steel production. You'll see more of this history on this hike around the Tannehill Ironworks Historical State Park.

The story of Tannehill begins in 1830 when Daniel Hillman came to Alabama from Pennsylvania and built a forge along Roupes Creek (aka Mud Creek), which was later purchased by local farmer Ninian Tannehill. With the use of slave labor, Tannehill supervised the construction of three tall furnaces, each built with large, hand-cut sandstone bricks.

By 1862 the ironworks was in full swing, producing pig iron for the Confederate army, but on March 31, 1865, the Eighth Iowa Cavalry of the US Army shelled and set fire to the foundry and torched the slave quarters.

The facility was eventually abandoned and soon overtaken by nature, which brings us to the 1970s when the State of Alabama and several colleges resurrected the site. Archaeological digs uncovered the old blower house and the main furnace. The furnace was rebuilt to its former glory and is now listed on the National Register of Historic Places.

The historical park is a fascinating place to just wander around. The streets are lined with forty historic structures of the period (1830 to 1870) that have been lovingly brought back to life and opened for the public to view. Along one section, local craftspeople demonstrate the making of quilts, furniture, and pottery between March and November. And of course, the restored furnace is the park's centerpiece.

You begin the hike at the Alabama Iron and Steel Museum. It will be well worth your while to spend some time in the museum and explore its many exhibits and artifacts that trace the history of Tannehill and Birmingham's iron and steel history.

The loop begins directly behind the museum next to Plank Road, which features cabins from the mid- to late 1800s. From there, four trails—the Iron Works Trail, Slave Quarters Road Trail, Old Bucksville Stage Road Trail, and Iron Haul Road—will lead you to the park's major historic sites. The trails will take you through thick oak and dogwood forests and alongside several creeks including Roupes Creek, which once helped power the furnace.

There is one trail intersection that causes a bit of confusion. After crossing the creek behind the museum, there is a Y. Take the left fork to the east (a sign here reads "Iron Works Trail"). The trail takes you past beautiful views of the creek, with several boiling rapids churning its blue-green waters, before taking you to the base of the furnace, an impressive sight. Take your time to stroll around the structure and take it all in.

From there, the trail joins the Slave Quarters Road Trail where the homes of the enslaved people who built and worked the furnace were once located; the Old Bucksville Stage Road Trail, which was the main highway into the area during the mid-1800s; and a short side trail to the slave cemetery. All that remain are simple, nameless rock headstones marking the graves.

You will return to the trailhead on the Iron Haul Road Trail where you'll catch nice views of the creek with some spots where you can sit and reflect in its waters.

While the trails are well-maintained dirt, gravel, and clay roads, after a good rain some of the route, especially the Iron Road returning to the trailhead, can be thick mud or have several water runoffs crossing it.

Miles and Directions

0.0   Start from behind the Alabama Iron and Steel Museum. Head down a set of cement stairs toward the creek to the southeast. Cross the creek on a small wooden bridge (a playground is on the opposite side of the creek on your right; a picnic area is to the left). There is a Y after the bridge. Take the left fork to the east (a sign here reads "Iron Works Trail"). This trail takes you behind the craft buildings and splendid views of the creek.

0.4   Arrive at the furnace. Cross the creek to the left (east) over the wood and steel Jim Folsom Bridge. On the other side come to the intersection with the Iron Haul Road Trail. A sign here points to the left (northeast), showing the way to the cemetery and Stage Road. Turn left here onto the Slave Quarters Road Trail.

0.5   Pass a short pier that juts into a pond to the left (west).

0.9   Cross a stream that flows under the road.

1.2   Come to the intersection with the Old Bucksville Stage Road Trail. A sign here points to the cemetery (to the right) and furnace (the way you just came). Turn right (southeast) onto the Old Bucksville Stage Road Trail.

1.9   Come to the intersection of the Iron Haul Road Trail and Cemetery Trail. Turn right (southwest) onto the Cemetery Trail.

2.0   Arrive at the slave cemetery. A chain-link fence encircles the site. You can enter through a gate that is tied shut with a

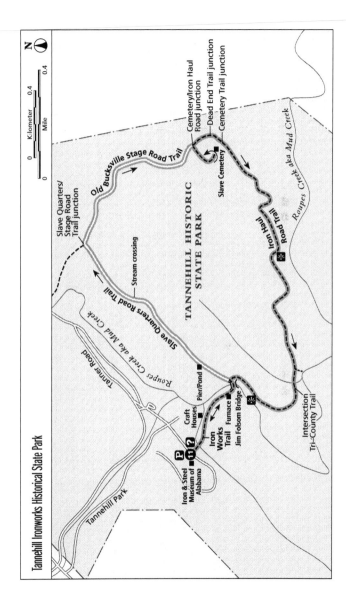

Tannehill Ironworks Historical State Park

rope. (**Option:** From the cemetery the trail continues to the southeast another 0.1 mile, where it connects with the Iron Haul Road Trail [mile 2.3 below]. On my last visit this section of trail was underwater with a runoff stream. I opted to turn around at the cemetery and return to the intersection of the Old Bucksville Stage Road and Iron Haul Road Trails.)

2.1 Back at the intersection of the three trails, turn right (southeast) onto the Iron Haul Road Trail.

2.2 Come to a Y. To the left (southeast) is a dead-end trail (and it's marked as such). Take the right fork (south).

2.3 Pass a side trail on the right (north). This is where the side trail from the cemetery joins the Iron Haul Road Trail. Continue straight (southwest).

2.8 Start seeing good views of Roupes Creek to the left (south).

3.3 A nice, grassy, 30-foot-long side trail leads to the banks of the creek.

3.4 Pass the Tri-County Trail coming in from the right (north). Continue straight to the west.

3.6 Good views of Roupes Creek to the left (west).

3.8 Return to the Jim Folsom Bridge. Retrace your steps to the parking lot.

4.1 Arrive back at the parking lot.

12 Ebenezer Swamp Ecological Preserve

This short but nature-packed, ADA accessible boardwalk hike leads you through a beautiful spring-fed tupelo swamp where the clear waters play host to a wide variety of wildlife you may see along the trail. Orchids, golden club, and Virginia sweetspire bloom in season, brightening the dark environment.

Start: Start from the gate in the fence to the northwest
Distance: 0.7-mile out-and-back
Hiking time: About 1 hour
Difficulty: Easy
Trail surface: ADA accessible boardwalk, some dirt and rock
Best season: Year-round
Other trail users: None
Canine compatibility: Dogs not permitted

Land status: University park
Schedule: Sunrise to sunset
Fess and permits: None
Maps: USGS Alabaster, AL
Contact: University of Montevallo Environmental Education Program, Harman Hall, Station 6480, Montevallo 35115; (205) 665-6463; www.montevallo.edu/campus-life/around-campus/ebenezer-swamp/

Finding the trailhead: From I-65 exit 234, take CR 87 southeast 0.3 mile and turn right onto Smokey Road/CR 12. Travel 1.6 mile and turn left on CR 24. Travel 0.4 mile and turn right onto Stagecoach Road. In less than 0.1 mile you will see a split rail fence on the left. Park next to the fence on the wide shoulder. Cross through the fence's gate. The trailhead is about 100 feet to the northwest and is well marked. **Trailhead GPS:** N33 11.070' / W87 01.471'

The Hike

While many tupelo swamps are disappearing due to development, a generous donation of sixty acres to the University of Montevallo has saved this nature-packed biosystem called the Ebenezer Swamp Ecological Preserve. The university created an ecological research and educational facility and opened a boardwalk through the heart of the swamp that you will be using for this hike.

The entirely ADA accessible hike begins in an upland mixed forest of pines and hardwoods on an old dirt and gravel road. Not long into the hike, you will pass a few impressive animal sculptures made out of old scrap steel by students.

Soon you will be on the boardwalk and walking atop the clear waters of the spring-fed swamp. Along the route you will see evidence of beaver—maybe even see one—and cross paths with turkey and deer. Orchids, golden club, and Virginia sweetspire are a few of the wildflowers that brighten the path in season.

Be sure to watch your step. The swamp is also the home of water moccasin, copperheads, and timber rattlers that may be sunning themselves along the trail.

Miles and Directions

0.0 Start from the parking area and head through the split rail fence to the northwest for 100 feet to the trailhead. There are restrooms here that may or may not be open and an information kiosk. The trail is a 5-foot-wide dirt and gravel path. In less than 0.1 mile, pass steel sculptures.

0.1 The boardwalk begins.

0.2 The boardwalk turns to the right. To the left there is a short boardwalk to a picnic table.

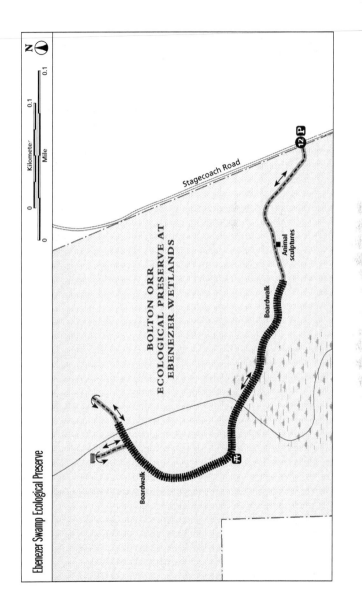

Ebenezer Swamp Ecological Preserve

0.3 Come to a Y. Take the left fork. In less than 0.1 mile, come to the end of the boardwalk. When ready, turn around and return to the Y and turn left to the northeast.

0.4 Come to the end of the boardwalk. Turn around and retrace your steps to the trailhead.

0.7 Arrive back at the trailhead.

13 Reflection Trail

This first visit to the Cahaba River takes you to the county park of the same name, where an easy walking 3.8-mile out-and-back is the perfect getaway for quiet solitude. While you only get glimpses of the river and the feeder Shades Creek with its swift shoals, the trail comes alive from March through mid-summer with beautiful wildflowers.

Start: Across the road from the pavilion to the west

Distance: 3.6-mile out-and-back with tail

Hiking time: About 2 hours

Difficulty: Easy

Trail surface: Dirt and rock

Best season: Year-round

Other trail users: Cyclists

Canine compatibility: Leashed dogs permitted

Land status: County preserve

Schedule: Sunrise to sunset

Fess and permits: None

Maps: USGS Halfmile Shoals, AL; trail maps available at trailhead kiosks or from the Forever Wild website (see Contact)

Contact: Alabama Forever Wild, 64 N. Union Street, Montgomery 36130; (334) 242-3484; www.alabamaforeverwild.com/cahaba-river-shelby-county-park; Discover Shelby County, 1301 County Services Drive, Pelham 35124; (205) 663-4542; shelbyal.com/Facilities/Facility/Details/Cahaba-River-Park-87

Finding the trailhead: From I-65 at exit 242 / CR 52, head west on CR 52 for 0.5 mile. Turn right onto Pelham Parkway / US 31 North. Travel 0.2 mile and turn left onto CR 52W. Travel 2.2 miles and turn left onto Helena Road / AL 261. In 0.8 mile, turn right to rejoin CR 52. In less than 0.1 mile at the first cross street, turn right to continue on CR 52. Travel 2.9 miles and turn left onto CR 13. Follow CR 13 for 7.8 miles and turn left onto River Road / CR 251. In 1.9 miles, turn right into Cahaba River Park. Follow the unnamed road for 0.9

mile and turn left onto another unnamed dirt road. Travel 0.2 mile. A pavilion with restrooms will be on the left with plenty of parking. Park here. The trail begins across the road to the west (signs lead the way). **Trailhead GPS:** N33 11.266' / W87 01.086'

The Hike

The Reflection Trail at Cahaba River Park is the perfect respite from the maddening world as it offers a bit of solitude from the bustling city.

This easy to slightly moderate 3.8-mile out-and-back leads you through a mixed pine and hardwood forest of white oak, green ash, and shagbark hickory to view the swift-flowing shoals of Shades Creek, a wide feeder of the Cahaba River itself. Along the route you will pass a few short-in-height outcroppings and a rocky bluff 20-feet above the creek.

On the way back, a short 0.2-mile side trail takes you to the popular canoe launch on the wide Cahaba River itself.

While the hike is just a nice ramble through the woods, it is especially nice in the spring when a variety of wildflowers bloom trailside including red buckeye, Piedmont azalea, and blue phlox, to name a few. The river and creek also play host to a wide variety of birds. Keep an eye out for belted kingfishers, Acadian flycatchers, red shouldered hawks, and a variety of warblers.

Miles and Directions

0.0 Start from the pavilion / parking area. Cross the road to the west to pick up the Reflection Trail. In less than 0.1 mile cross a wide dirt road. Signs lead the way.

0.7 A side trail leads to the Cahaba River and a canoe launch. You'll come back to this later. Continue straight.

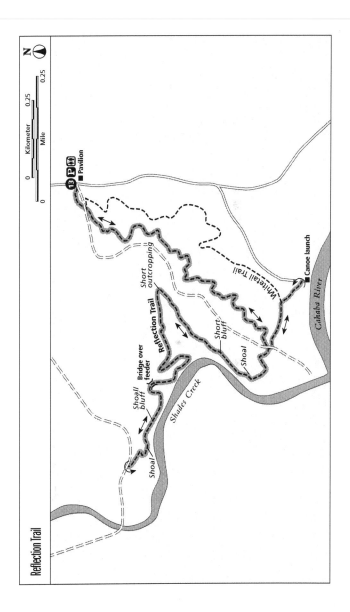

Reflection Trail

0.8 Come to first fast shoal in Shade Creek. Best viewed in winter.

0.9 Pass a short rock bluff below trail.

1.1 Pass a short rock outcropping.

1.5 Cross a 15-foot wooden bridge over feeder.

1.6 Pass another swift shoal in the creek viewed from a bluff 20 feet above the creek. In less than 0.1 mile, pass another shoal.

1.7 Come to a sign pointing the direction to Shades Creek and the Reflection Trail back the way you came. Turn around and begin retracing your steps.

2.7 Back at the side trail from mile 0.7, take the right fork to head to the canoe launch and Cahaba River. At the Y, take the right fork.

2.8 Arrive at the Cahaba River. When ready, retrace your steps back to mile 2.7.

2.9 Turn right (northeast) and head back to the trailhead.

3.6 Arrive back at the trailhead.

14 Falling Rock Falls

Only 40 miles south of Birmingham there is a small, relatively unknown wildlife management area where a leisurely walk down a gravel road, past new-growth pines, leads you to a hidden surprise that (so far) only locals know about—a 90-foot plunge waterfall known as Falling Rock Falls.

Start: At the trailhead behind a steel gate on the west end of the parking area
Distance: 1.8-mile out-and-back
Hiking time: About 1 hour
Difficulty: Moderate
Trail surface: Gravel road, dirt and rock footpath
Best season: Sept to May
Other trail users: None

Canine compatibility: Leashed dogs permitted
Land status: Wildlife management area
Schedule: Sunrise to sunset
Fess and permits: None
Maps: USGS Pea Ridge, AL
Contact: Calera Gas Co. LLC, Eddings Town Rd., Montevallo 35115; (205) 665-0322; www.caleragas.com

Finding the trailhead: From Montevallo at the intersection of College Drive and Middle Street, head northwest on Middle Street 0.6 mile and turn right onto CR17. Travel 3.2 miles and turn left onto CR22 West. Travel 2.3 miles and the dirt and gravel pull-off for parking will be on the right with room for fifteen cars comfortably and plenty of room to pull far enough away from the road. Do not block the gate.
Trailhead GPS: N33 09.952' / W86 53.960'

The Hike

Hidden away in the small and relatively unknown Lanier Wildlife Management Area is a 90-foot gem of a waterfall,

Falling Rock Falls. The ribbon of water from Eddings Creek courses over the rocky ledge forming a nice shallow pool below; a deep rock shelter formed by the falls allows you to walk behind the watery curtain.

The only drawback to this magnificent flow is that, unfortunately, some who visit believe that the walls of the rock shelter were put there to display their personal "artwork"—graffiti.

This trek begins at the dirt and gravel pull-off on CR 22 by walking around the right side of the steel gate that blocks the gravel road that comprises most of the hike. Don't worry. You will have a chance to duck into the woods in a bit.

You will encounter three forks in the road along the route. At the second one at mile 0.5, you will pass a pretty, little wetland on the left and later at the third Y, you will pass yet another little wetland where you will be serenaded by frog song after a good rain.

Eventually, you will leave the gravel road at mile 0.7 and come to a 4-foot-wide side trail into the woods on the left. The short dirt footpath soon becomes a wide clay and rock path (it's actually a run-off channel). Be careful along this section. The flat rocks and clay can be slick during and after rain.

Once you arrive at Eddings Creek you will be at the top of the falls. Use caution here. The edge and drop-off can be deceiving. From here, the path is not well defined, but it is to your right and follows the south rim of the gorge where you will get your first look at the falls through the trees. There is a nondescript trail on the left that heads steeply down into the gorge using switchbacks and ends at the base of the falls. Again, use caution heading down the steep slope.

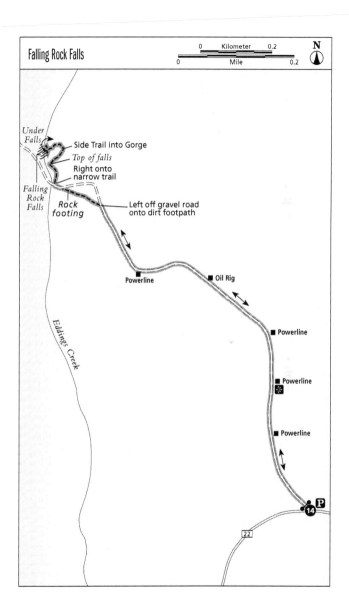

Falling Rock Falls

	Kilometer	
0		0.2
0	Mile	0.2

N

Under
Falls

Side Trail into Gorge

Top of falls

Right onto
narrow trail

Falling
Rock
Falls

*Rock
footing*

Left off gravel road
onto dirt footpath

Eddings Creek

Powerline

■ Oil Rig

■ Powerline

■ Powerline

■ Powerline

P
14

22

Miles and Directions

0.0 Start at the steel gate by walking around the gate on the right side.

0.1 Cross under powerlines.

0.2 Cross under powerlines.

0.3 The road forks. Take the left fork to the northwest.

0.4 Pass an oil rig on the right.

0.6 Take the right fork in the road to the northwest.

0.7 Turn off road onto a narrow, non-blazed dirt path into the woods on the left.

0.8 The trail widens out and is a flat rock. Use caution when there is water running down its face. In less than 0.1 mile, turn right onto a narrow dirt and rock path. In a few yards, arrive at the top of the falls. Continue on the narrow footpath along the gorge rim to the right (north).

0.9 Carefully take a nondescript trail to the left and begin heading steeply down into the gorge. In less than 0.1 mile, arrive at the base of the falls and the rock shelter. When ready, turn around and retrace your steps back to the trailhead.

1.8 Arrive back at the trailhead.

15 Furnace Trail

A nice, easy walk in the woods at Brierfield Ironworks Historical State Park leads us to another one of the productive iron furnaces from central Alabama's past. The park's Furnace Trail takes us past the remains of the Bibb Furnace as well as the reservoir that once fed water to the massive structure.

Start: From the parking area just past the main entrance at the park office
Distance: 1.4-mile lollipop
Hiking time: About 1 hour
Difficulty: Easy
Trail surface: Dirt and gravel footpaths, minimal asphalt
Best season: Year-round
Other trail users: None

Canine compatibility: Leashed dogs permitted
Land status: Historical state park
Schedule: Sunrise to sunset
Fess and permits: Day-use fee
Maps: USGS Aldridge, AL
Contact: Brierfield Ironworks Historical State Park, 240 Furnace Parkway, Brierfield 35035; (205) 665-1856; www.brierfield ironworks.org/

Finding the trailhead: From the intersection of AL 195 and AL 25 in Montevallo take AL 25 south 6.6 miles. Turn left onto Frederick Pass. Travel 0.4 mile and turn left onto Furnace Parkway. In 0.1 mile come to the entrance gate and pay station. If no one is staffing the gate, deposit your day-use fee in the honor box. Continue straight another 0.1 mile and find a parking spot. This is where you will start this hike. **Trailhead GPS:** N33 02.313' / W86 56.902'

The Hike

This is a good angle from where you can better see how the state is working to preserve the furnace remains and where they are excavating to uncover more of the structure. When ready continue on the trail to the northwest. The trail is once again a narrow dirt path.

This easy trek allows you to view more of the Birmingham area's rich steel history as you venture to the Brierfield Ironworks Historical State Park and take a nice walk in the woods to view the remains of the Bibb Furnace on the Furnace Trail.

Bibb Furnace was once a major supplier of pig iron to locals and later the Confederate military. It was a unique business venture. When speculators came to Alabama to make their fortune in the burgeoning iron industry, they usually had some semblance of knowledge about the business. Bibb was bankrolled and built by a group of men who called their venture the Bibb County Iron Company.

The company was led by Caswell Campbell Huckabee who admittedly had no clue about the iron industry. With the exception of a forge operator from Six Mile, Alabama, Jonathan Smith, Huckabee's partners were either farmers or grist mill operators.

In 1862 the stone furnace was completed and actually began producing high grade iron. The Confederate military wanted to place orders for the iron but at a much lower price than private businesses, so the partners refused to sell to the military. Later that year, the Confederate States of America (CSA) passed a law that would require furnaces like Bibb to produce a certain quantity of iron for the war effort. Huckabee agreed to produce 1,000 tons of pig iron for the military in exchange for an advance of $20,000 in Confederate bonds.

Soon, the CSA gave Huckabee a "choice": give them all the iron produced at the furnace, sell or lease the furnace to the government, or have the entire operation confiscated. Huckabee chose to sell the furnace for $600,000, nine slaves, twenty carts, twenty wheelbarrows, two hundred axes, forty-one oxen, and seventy mules. This would be the only furnace owned by the Confederate government.

In March 1865 as the Civil War was nearing its end, the walls of the furnace came tumbling down as the Union army, vowing to destroy the South's "power to make war" laid the furnace complex to waste.

In 1976, the site was put under the protection of the Bibb County Historical Society who erected a protective cover over the remains of the site and opened Brierfield Ironworks Historical State Park. And here we are.

Almost immediately after entering the park you will see a sign marked "Furnace Trail" on your left and you may wonder why I didn't start the hike there at the official trailhead. In all my visits to Brierfield I have encountered campers set up for the weekend in front of the trailhead, so instead of trampling through their campsites, I opted to start on the far northern end of the campground where a side trail leads in.

This short hike through the forest, which is magnificent in the fall, will take you past the impressive sight of the ruins from its base and from above and up to the top of a ridge to view the reservoir that once provided water for furnace operations.

The trail is not marked but, for the most part, is easy to follow. However, at several intersections you may get confused about which way to go. Don't worry—most of these side trails simply loop around back onto the main trail.

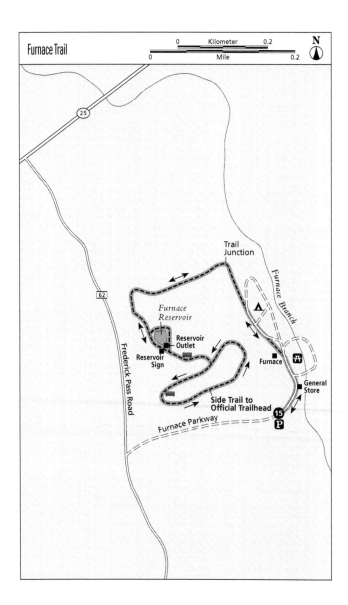

N

0   Kilometer   0.2

0   Mile   0.2

25

62

Trail
Junction

Furnace Branch

*Furnace
Reservoir*

Reservoir
Outlet

Reservoir
Sign

Furnace

Frederick Pass Road

General
Store

Side Trail to
Official Trailhead

15
P

Furnace Parkway

Miles and Directions

0.0   Start from the parking area just past and to the right of the entrance shack. Head to the north on the paved road heading toward the furnace. On the way you will pass the country store and a small picnic area on the right. In less than 0.1 mile, come to the furnace remains and a Y. Take the left fork to the northwest onto a wide gravel road that rounds the left side of the campground.

0.1   With the campground on the right, turn left (northwest) off the gravel road onto an old, wide dirt service road.

0.2   Come to an intersection. Turn left (southwest) onto the narrow dirt footpath.

0.3   Come to a Y. Take the right fork to the west. In less than 0.1 mile come to an intersection. Turn left (south) onto the wide dirt path.

0.4   Come to the furnace reservoir, a depression with a sealed-off outlet is on the opposite side. Walk around the reservoir to the opposite side. There are four benches here.

0.5   Two trails fork behind the reservoir sign. Take the left fork to the east, counterclockwise around the loop. In less than 0.1 mile, pass a bench on the left.

0.6   Come to an intersection at a clearing. In the clearing is a bench. Turn right (southwest) onto a narrow dirt path.

0.7   Continue straight, passing a side trail to the right.

0.8   Come to the backside of the furnace. A fence here with a "Do Not Enter" sign keeps visitors from venturing down.

0.9   Arrive back at the clearing and retrace your steps back to the trailhead.

1.4   Arrive back at the trailhead.

16 Piper Interpretive Trail

The Cahaba River, one of the most ecologically diverse rivers in the country, is the setting for this hike. This 2.8-mile out-and-back takes you through a cathedral of towering pines culminating in breathtaking views of the rapids and the river itself from high above on rocky bluffs.

Start: West side of parking lot behind the gate
Distance: 2.8-mile out-and-back
Hiking time: About 1.5 hours
Difficulty: Moderate with steady climbs to overlooks
Trail surface: Dirt and rock
Best season: Fall, when the hardwoods blaze with color
Other trail users: None
Canine compatibility: Leashed dogs permitted

Land status: National wildlife refuge
Schedule: Sunrise to sunset
Fess and permits: None
Maps: USGS West Blocton East, AL
Contact: Cahaba National Wildlife Refuge, 407 Baby Bains Gap Road, Anniston 36205; (256) 848-6833; www.fws.gov/refuge/cahaba-river

Finding the trailhead: From the intersection of Middle Street and AL 25 in Montevallo take AL 25 South 8.6 miles. Turn right onto Bulldog Bend Road (CR 65). Travel 5.9 miles and turn left onto Bibb County 24 / Cahaba River Drive. Travel 1.2 miles. The parking lot and trailhead will be on the left. It's a little hard to see so keep your eyes peeled. **Trailhead GPS:** N33 05.291' / W87 02.917'

The Hike

The Cahaba River that winds its way through Birmingham has been recognized by scientists as one of the most ecologically diverse rivers in the country.

The river is the longest free-flowing river in the state and has been identified as having more species of fish than in the entire state of California, 131 to be exact. In all, sixty-four rare and unique plants and animals can be found in and around these waters including thirteen that can't be found anywhere else in the world. The most famous plant that grows in the river is the Cahaba lily, with its delicate, snowy white petals. The lily requires a special environment to thrive: a fast moving, rocky river. It can only be found in three places—Georgia, South Carolina, and here on the Cahaba River.

While many people love to paddle the Cahaba to see the flowers in bloom and shoot the shoals, this hike will take you on a journey for a fresh look at the river—from high above on rocky bluffs.

This hike is located in the 3,000-acre Cahaba River National Wildlife Refuge and uses the Piper Interpretive Trail, a 2.8-mile out-and-back hike up the rocky ridges lining the river. The first 0.7 mile is accessible but after that, it becomes a moderate climb unsuitable for people with severe disabilities.

The trail begins by meandering through a thick hardwood forest that provides a respite from the summer sun and is stunning in the fall when it blazes with color. Soon you will be walking through a cathedral of towering pines, their needles covering the path providing soft footing. Many birds including wood thrushes, Kentucky warblers, and great-crested flycatchers serenade you as you walk.

Soon, you'll notice a change in the terrain as the path gets rockier and steeper as it climbs to the top of a ridge. From here you will come to three platforms where you will get spectacular views of the river itself and its fast-moving shoals.

The third overlook is the turnaround for the hike. Just past the overlook, it looks like the trail continues, and it does, heading back to the trailhead, but it is a really difficult gravel road to walk with large 3- to 4-inch gravel stones. That's why we made this hike an out-and-back.

The parking lot is hidden away so go slowly as you approach it or you might miss it. It is a wide gravel lot that can hold fifty cars easily.

Miles and Directions

0.0 Start at the kiosk on the northwest side of the parking lot. There is a metal gate here. You'll see a gravel road heading to the left (west) and a dirt path to the right. Take the dirt path to the northwest. In less than 0.1 mile, begin heading steeply downhill through a series of switchbacks.

0.1 Cross a 40-foot bridge over a run-off area.

0.2 Pass interpretive signs about songbirds and snakes and a bench.

0.4 Cross straight across a fire lane to the west.

0.5 Pass a bench on the left.

0.8 Pass a bench on the left.

0.9 Pass a trail direction sign pointing back the way you came. Keep going straight to the southwest.

1.2 A side trail heads off to the right (west) steeply down the hill to a platform for an excellent view of the shoals of the Cahaba River far below. Continue on the main trail

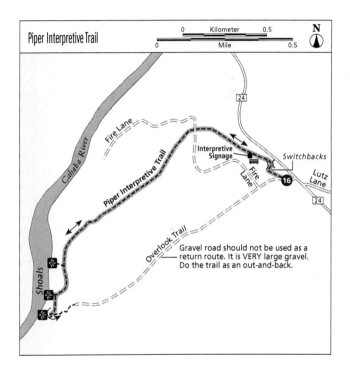

Piper Interpretive Trail

N

0   Kilometer   0.5

0   Mile   0.5

Cahaba River

Fire Lane

Piper Interpretive Trail

Interpretive Signage

Switchbacks

Fire Lane

Lutz Lane

24

24

16

Overlook Trail

Shoals

Gravel road should not be used as a return route. It is VERY large gravel. Do the trail as an out-and-back.

to the south. In less than 0.1 mile, cross a bridge over a seasonal stream.

1.3 Another side trail on the right heads steeply down to a rock bluff for a river view. Use caution on the bluff.

1.4 You will come to a sign pointing to the left and right (north/south). Turn to the right for a final look at the river. When done, turn around and retrace your steps back to the trailhead.

2.8 Arrive back at the trailhead.

17 Hurricane Creek Park

Explore the geologic and watery features of Hurricane Creek Park. This moderate to difficult 2.2-mile double loop with extension begins atop a ridge and winds its way down to the park's namesake creek, passing beneath tall rock bluffs, rock shelters that invite exploring, and waterfalls you can walk behind. In the valley there is the perfect swimming hole and a walk along the Creek Trail with tumbling shoals and wildflowers in season.

Start: From the patio at the old building to the east

Distance: 2.2-mile loop with extension

Hiking time: About 2 hours

Difficulty: Hurricane Trail: Difficult; Creek Trail: Easy; North Highland Ridge Trail: Moderate

Trail surface: Packed dirt, rocks, some stone stairs

Best season: Fall through spring for waterfalls, summer for swimming

Other trail users: None

Canine compatibility: Leashed dogs permitted

Land status: City preserve

Schedule: Sunrise to sunset

Fess and permits: None

Maps: USGS Falkville, AL

Contact: Hurricane Creek Park, 22600 US Highway 31 North, Vinemont 35179; (256) 734-9157; www.cullmanrecreation.org/hurricane-creek-park15903d77

Finding the trailhead: From the intersection of I-65 at exit 308 and US 278 / 4th Street SW in Cullman, head east on US 278 / 4th Street SW for 1.4 miles. Stay to the left at the fork onto Main Avenue SW. Travel 0.6 mile and turn left onto US 31 N / 2nd Avenue NW. Travel 7.9 miles and the parking lot will be on the right. There is a building to the southeast. Walk to the building and walk around the right side crossing a patio. This is the trailhead. **Trailhead GPS:** N34 17.206' / W86 53.698'

The Hike

This challenging hike takes you to the town of Falkville where you will find a wonderland of geology and waterfalls that makes for an amazing day hike—Hurricane Creek Park.

We will use four trails—the Hurricane, South Ridge, North Highland Ridge, and Creek Trails—to form this 2.2-mile double-loop with an extension along Hurricane Creek that juts out like a tail from the main double loop.

This is a beautiful hike over extremely rocky dirt footpath. The geology is remarkable with tall sandstone bluffs lining much of the path, their faces weathered away over the centuries by nature. Several seasonal creeks cascade down these rock walls forming deep rock shelters where you can walk behind the waterfalls. One of the most impressive falls is on the return trip where you cross all three tiers of the cascade over wooden bridges. Remember, these waterfalls are seasonal and best viewed from fall through spring when the rains fill the channels.

The trek holds a couple of surprises like the Twilight Tunnel, a long—and very dark—tunnel or cave through a rock jumble. If you are afraid of the dark or caves, the Bypass Trail takes you around the tunnel to the other side.

There is also the Bottleneck, a very narrow cut in a boulder you could shimmy through, but a sign there tells you to go around it. Heed that sign.

The centerpiece of the park is Hurricane Creek itself, a wide rushing creek that flows into the park's picnic area where an old dam has created a wonderful swimming hole, a local favorite.

THE TEN ESSENTIALS OF HIKING

American Hiking Society

Whether you plan to be gone for a couple of hours or several months, make sure to pack these items. Become familiar with these items and know how to use them.

1. Appropriate Footwear
Happy feet make for pleasant hiking. Think about traction, support, and protection when selecting well-fitting shoes or boots.

2. Navigation

While phones and GPS units are handy, they aren't always reliable in the backcountry; consider carrying a paper map and compass as a backup and know how to use them.

3. Water (and a way to purify it)

As a guideline, plan for half a liter of water per hour in moderate temperatures/terrain. Carry enough water for your trip and know where and how to treat water while you're out on the trail.

4. Food

Pack calorie-dense foods to help fuel your hike, and carry an extra portion in case you are out longer than expected.

5. Rain Gear & Dry-Fast Layers

The weatherman is not always right. Dress in layers to adjust to changing weather and activity levels. Wear moisture-wicking clothes and carry a warm hat.

6. Safety Items (light, fire, and a whistle)
Have means to start an emergency fire, signal for help, and see the trail and your map in the dark.

7. First Aid Kit
Supplies to treat illness or injury are only as helpful as your knowledge of how to use them. Take a class to gain the skills needed to administer first aid and CPR.

8. Knife or Multi-Tool
With countless uses, a multi-tool can help with gear repair and first aid.

9. Sun Protection
Sunscreen, sunglasses, and sun-protective clothing should be used in every season regardless of temperature or cloud cover.

10. Shelter
Protection from the elements in the event you are injured or stranded is necessary. A lightweight, inexpensive space blanket is a great option.

Find other helpful resources at AmericanHiking.org/hiking-resources.

About the Author

Author and freelance writer **Joe Cuhaj** has been hiking since he was a teenager growing up in the mountains of northern New Jersey and New York State in the 1970s. He moved to Alabama in 1980 with his wife, Maggie, and immediately fell in love with the state's rich biodiversity, its stunning waterfalls, breathtaking views, dark and mysterious bayous, and historic sites. He penned his first guide to hiking the state—*Hiking Alabama*—in 2000. It is now in its fifth edition. Since that time, Joe has written five additional Alabama outdoor recreation guides for Falcon. He has also written four historic nonfiction titles including *Space Oddities: Forgotten Stories of Mankind's Exploration of Space*. Learn more about Joe's other books on his website, www.joe-cuhaj.com.

0.1 mile, cross the creek over a bridge and on the other side turn left (northeast) onto the Creek Trail.

1.2   Come to a bridge and cross the creek on the bridge to the northeast. On the other side, turn right (northeast) and continue along the creek. In spring and summer, the path is lined with brightly colored wildflowers.

1.5   Pass another bridge on the right. This is the turnaround for the Creek Trail. Retrace your steps to the bridge at mile 1.2.

1.8   Back at the same bridge from mile 1.2, turn right to the north and you will see the sign that reads "High Trail Long Way Back to Park." Continue north. Shortly the trail swings to the left (northwest).

1.9   Pass another weeping bluff on the right. In less than 0.1 mile, pass a waterfall on the right. From here there is another set of sharp switchbacks uphill. At the end of the first switchback, cross a long bridge over a tier of the waterfall.

2.0   Come to the end of the switchbacks and walk past the top of the waterfall. In less than 0.1 mile, at the top of the ridge, the trail turns sandy with some rocks but levels out. Arrive at a sandstone natural bridge on the right.

2.1   Come to the upper end of a cement road. Turn right onto the road, following it only about 100 feet where the trail veers off the road to the left (southwest). Stay on the trail. In less than 0.1 mile, cross a narrow 60-foot-long bridge over a drop-off.

2.2   Pass a side trail on left that goes straight down to the picnic area. In less than 0.1 mile, cross a 150-foot bridge over a fast-moving stream. In less than 0.1 mile, arrive back at the trailhead.

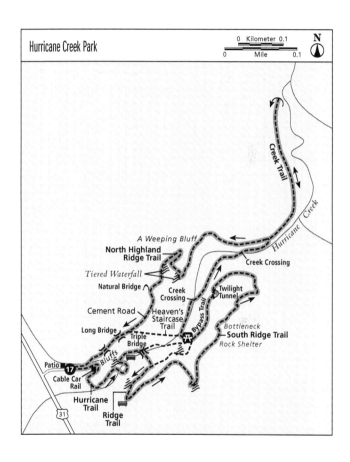

Hurricane Creek Park

0   Kilometer   0.1
0   Mile   0.1

N

Creek Trail

Hurricane Creek

A Weeping Bluff

North Highland
Ridge Trail

Creek Crossing

Tiered Waterfall

Natural Bridge

Creek
Crossing

Twilight
Tunnel

Cement Road

Heaven's
Staircase
Trail

Bypass Trail

Bottleneck
South Ridge Trail

Long Bridge

Triple
Bridge

Rock Shelter

Bluffs

Patio

17

Cable Car
Rail

Hurricane
Trail

31

Ridge
Trail

From here, the Creek Trail—which parallels Hurricane Creek—offers beautiful wildflowers like dwarf iris, buttonbush, and red cardinals in the spring, brightening the path as it meanders through a forest with oak leaf hydrangea and tulip poplars.

The hike described here begins by taking a right from the trailhead onto the Hurricane Trail. It is a very steep and rocky downhill climb to the creek and is rated difficult. Use your best judgment if hiking with small children and dogs. The remainder of the hike is easy to moderate.

To make it easier, an option would be to avoid the Hurricane Trail altogether and instead start by going straight on the North Highland Ridge Trail then across Heaven's Staircase Trail to the picnic area described at mile 1.1 and avoiding the south loop altogether. This trail is rated as moderate and uses a series of switchbacks to help you down, making the walk much easier. Once at the picnic area you can continue with the Miles and Directions as described.

Miles and Directions

0.0 Start just behind the building in the parking lot on the right side at the patio. Shortly, the trail forks. Turn right (east) onto the Hurricane Trail. (**FYI:** This is a difficult trail with a steep, rock-strewn climb down to Hurricane Creek.) In less than 0.1 mile, pass an abandoned cable car rail on the right.

0.2 To your left, impressive rock bluffs begin and soon you will be walking through a rock shelter behind a two-tier (seasonal) waterfall. In less than 0.1 mile, a trail splits off to the right with a sign reading "To Twilight Tunnel / South Ridge Trail." Turn right (southeast) here.

1.1 Arrive at the picnic area with the beautiful, low, cascading falls of a dam and a deep, cold swimming hole. From here take a right (northwest) onto the High Trail. In less than